Doctor in the House

A Comedy in Three Acts

by Ted Willis

from the novel by
Richard Gordon

A Samuel French Acting Edition

FOUNDED 1830
New York Hollywood London Toronto
SAMUELFRENCH.COM

Copyright © 1957 by Richard Gordon and Ted Willis

ALL RIGHTS RESERVED

CAUTION: Professionals and amateurs are hereby warned that *DOCTOR IN THE HOUSE* is subject to a royalty. It is fully protected under the copyright laws of the United States of America, the British Commonwealth, including Canada, and all other countries of the Copyright Union. All rights, including professional, amateur, motion picture, recitation, lecturing, public reading, radio broadcasting, television and the rights of translation into foreign languages are strictly reserved. In its present form the play is dedicated to the reading public only.

The amateur live stage performance rights to *DOCTOR IN THE HOUSE* are controlled exclusively by Samuel French, Inc., and royalty arrangements and licenses must be secured well in advance of presentation. PLEASE NOTE that amateur royalty fees are set upon application in accordance with your producing circumstances. When applying for a royalty quotation and license please give us the number of performances intended, dates of production, your seating capacity and admission fee. Royalties are payable one week before the opening performance of the play to Samuel French, Inc., at 45 W. 25th Street, New York, NY 10010.

Royalty of the required amount must be paid whether the play is presented for charity or gain and whether or not admission is charged.

Stock royalty quoted upon application to Samuel French, Inc.

For all other rights than those stipulated above, apply to: Curtis Brown Ltd., 347 Madison Avenue, New York, N.Y. 10017.

Particular emphasis is laid on the question of amateur or professional readings, permission and terms for which must be secured in writing from Samuel French, Inc.

Copying from this book in whole or in part is strictly forbidden by law, and the right of performance is not transferable.

Whenever the play is produced the following notice must appear on all programs, printing and advertising for the play: "Produced by special arrangement with Samuel French, Inc."

Due authorship credit must be given on all programs, printing and advertising for the play.

No one shall commit or authorize any act or omission by which the copyright of, or the right to copyright, this play may be impaired.

No one shall make any changes in this play for the purpose of production.

Publication of this play does not imply availability for performance. Both amateurs and professionals considering a production are strongly advised in their own interests to apply to Samuel French, Inc., for written permission before starting rehearsals, advertising, or booking a theatre.

No part of this book may be reproduced, stored in a retrieval system, or transmitted in any form, by any means, now known or yet to be invented, including mechanical, electronic, photocopying, recording, videotaping, or otherwise, without the prior written permission of the publisher.

ISBN 978-0-573-60811-7   Printed in U.S.A.   #607

DOCTOR IN THE HOUSE was first presented in London at the Victoria Palace Theatre on 30th July, 1956 with the following cast of characters:

TONY GRIMSDYKE, *a medical student* ... ..*Alan White*
SIMON SPARROW, *a medical student* ... .*Philip Gilbert*
JOHN EVANS, *a medical student* .*Edward Woodward*
VERA, *a lady-in-waiting* .... *Sonya Cordeau*
BROMLEY, *a hospital porter* ....*Douglas Ives*
SIR LANCELOT SPRATT, *a surgeon* ....*Frank Thring*
MISS WINSLOW (RIGGIE), *a nurse* .. . *Anthea Askey*
THE MATRON, *a battleship* ....*Elizabeth Alys*
JANET, *a nurse* .. ..*Jennifer Wright*

The play was directed by Richard Bird with settings by John Russell.

The action of the play takes place in the lodgings of the medical students.

ACT ONE

SCENE 1: The flat, one evening.

SCENE 2. The flat, a few days later. Evening.

ACT TWO

The flat, two years later, a day or so before Christmas.
Evening.

ACT THREE

SCENE 1 The flat, two years later.

SCENE 2: The flat, the following evening.

PRODUCTION NOTE

DOCTOR IN THE HOUSE is essentially light-hearted and there are very few passages which should not be played all out for comedy—even when the boys are in dire trouble. The dialogue is mostly throw-away stuff and little success will come from working too hard for laughs. Despite their facetiousness the three young men must not be burlesqued give the dialogue a chance and apply the "student rag" atmosphere in subtle doses.

As always, casting requires great care. Tony should be as good-looking as possible; an exuberant, carefree fellow who is a natural leader. When he is downcast he goes the whole hog and is more amusing than ever. During his amorous demonstrations with Vera he should be quite uninhibited, behaving as though no one else were present. His appearances before the curtain must be full of charm; he should woo the audience in a casual, almost off-hand, manner, insinuating them into his confidence. Let him behave as though talking to two or three people in a bar.

During the action of the play Simon develops from a callow youth into a sophisticated young man and this delineation of character affords plenty of scope for one of your more experienced actors. (Whatever you do, don't cast a callow youth to play the part.) Even with the onset of worldliness a certain fundamental ingenuousness should remain with Simon throughout and his prowess as a rugger player should be emphasized by his burly good looks. He is terrified of his uncle, Sir Lancelot, and this should be all the more laughter-making because of his fearlessness in other directions.

John Edwards has the hardest task of the three students. This actor should be a really fine team-player for, time after time, he has to hold things together. His tolerance of Tony's wild ideas is always droll, but it is not long before he finds himself joining in wholeheartedly. In my production he smoked four different pipes during the three acts—each one eccentric.

In my opinion, Vera should be played as a Continental. This gives her a slight element of mystery and fascination and provides the play with a certain "lift." She should be frank, open and in no way a coquette. She can be very spirited at times and can give Tony as good as he gives her. Undoubtedly in love with him, she is quite delighted whenever he becomes demonstrative, enjoying and reciprocating his embraces. Her duologue with Simon at the opening of Act I, Scene 2 should be played as a bit of fun. She sets out to flirt a little because she knows his embarrassment will amuse her The keynote of the scene is Vera's line, "Poor Simon, it isn't right to tease you like this." When John returns from his first confinement in Act II she should play with absolute sincerity.

Bromley is an unmistakable cockney but his accent should not be too thick. His offer to help Simon in Act I is quite sincere and funnier in consequence. His medical examination of him in Act II, helped by Tony, should be conducted in a most serious manner for Bromley considers that his many years' experience as porter at the hospital have virtually qualified him as a doctor. Nevertheless, he is extremely scared during the operation scene and it is important that the tremendous howl before he passes out should be of sufficient volume to bring Riggie and Vera from the bedroom. In the drama rehearsal Bromley is the most ardent of the players, hamming his part in old-fashioned melodramatic style, but in the final scene he should give a perfect performance in the plot to deceive the Matron and Janet. He should look fifty or thereabouts and must be careful not to over-act this well-written character part.

In this kind of broad comedy it is quite legitimate to cast to type and, if you have anything approaching a real-life Sir Lancelot among your members, the part will play itself. When he is on the stage he should dominate it, he treats everyone else as though they were still in the kindergarten. Choose, if possible, a tall prosperous-looking man and give him a beard. It must be quite obvious from his appearance and bearing that he is a success at his job and he should have a deep, penetrating voice as he spends most of his time topping the laughs. The actor playing this part should have a great sense of comedy although he should never suggest that he is trying to be funny.

Riggie is an eccentric type: simple and dumb, as the script denotes. Her best moments are in the drama rehearsal when she proves to be a very bad actress indeed and, what's more, hates it. The Matron should be a formidable character, played by a big woman. There should be an acid bite in her booming voice but, in the final scene, it must be borne in mind that there is another side to her character, the aunt-in-law to be. Her attempts to de-frost herself are never quite successful but the smacking kiss she lands on Simon's lips is delightful.

Janet is a rewarding part. There is a very business-like streak in her character, she knows what she wants and is determined to get it. We played her as a prudish-cum-horsey type (probably from South Kensington) and it proved very successful. The actress must be careful to preserve the right balance in her long duologue with Simon. In the last scene she is in a difficult position and must play with a sincere bewilderment which gradually turns to anger.

The setting provides little difficulty and groups with a small stage have a definite advantage as an intimate atmosphere is essential throughout the play. To denote the passage of time, changes should be made in the "trophies" and, perhaps, in the position of the furniture. (The settee and large table must not be too heavy as they have to be moved during the action of the play.) The curtains should be practical and, if possible, there should be a practical light just inside each bedroom door which the actors switch on and off when going in and out.

PRODUCTION NOTE

A curtain over the window seat makes a convenient place for certain props, such as the sherry and the bowl for the cocktail, which should be as large as possible and made of glass so that the audience can see the mixture change colour. (The advocaat is made of custard, of course.)

The exposition scene (Act I, Scene 1) beginning with Tony's line, "You may not know it, Simon, but your uncle is the lord of St. Swithin's," should be taken at a spanking pace, except for the few pauses indicated, until the re-entrance of Vera with the beer. Let the laughs look after themselves.

The duologue between Simon and Janet in Act II, Scene 1 should be played in a subdued light—supposedly from the small lamp on the table. The other lights are switched off by Tony when he goes out with Vera and John. The fun in this scene is hilarious but care must be taken by the producer that it does not get out of hand.

It is most important that at the beginning of the "plot" scene, i.e. the entrance of John in Act III, Scene 2 his clicking noise and wink to Simon should get over to the audience, putting them in the know. From here to the end the play is brimful of laughter. The producer should obtain the advice of a doctor friend on the correct pronunciation of the medical terms, which must trip off the tongue.

A word about curtains: Act I, Scene 1, fast; Act I, Scene 2, medium (a picture curtain may be taken here—dance continuing); Act II, fast; Act III, Scene 1, medium to slow; Act III, Scene 2, very slow. (At the producer's discretion the picture curtain may be cut. I think this stimulates the applause.)

If you are about to be associated with this play you will find its preparation great fun and good luck to you.

RICHARD BIRD

Doctor in the House

PROLOGUE

The house-lights are still on as the Stage Manager appears through tabs and addresses the audience:—

S.M. Ladies and gentlemen . . . We are very sorry to say that there will be a short delay before we can begin our play tonight. Unfortuantely our leading lady, Miss Dawn Grey, has . . . er . . . met with a slight accident. Nothing serious, but she must receive some medical attention before we can continue . . . Is there a doctor in the house?

SIMON. (*From somewhere in the audience.*) I'm a doctor.

TONY. (*From somewhere in the audience.*) So am I.

S.M. Would you come up, please, sir?

(*There is a commotion from the audience and* TONY GRIMSDYKE *and* SIMON SPARROW *converge on the stage from opposite sides and climb on to the boards.* TONY *to the* L. SIMON *to the* R.)

SIMON. Where is she?

TONY. I was here first.

SIMON. Now look here . . . Tony! Tony Grimsdyke!

TONY. Simon Sparrow! (*Crossing in front of the* S.M. *to* SIMON.) Simon, you dogsbody . . . Well, well . . .

(*They pommel each other affectionately.*)

S.M. If one of you gentlemen . . .

TONY. Just a moment, old chap. (*To* SIMON.) You don't look a day older . . .

SIMON. You haven't changed much yourself.

TONY. Ah, that's all you know. I'm a serious G.P. now.

SIMON. Whereabouts? Up north?

TONY. Fathead! In Mayfair. That's the place, my boy. They still like a bit of manners with their medicine and they don't mind coughing up . . . How about you?

SIMON. General practice too. Down at Lawley New housing estate. Tough going.

TONY. You're the sort of bloke who gives medicine a good name. How's the old sex life these days?

SIMON. So-so. I'm kept pretty busy, you know . . .

S.M. (*Holds the center opening of the curtain for one of them to go through.*) Please . . . I hate to interrupt.

TONY. Look, old boy, you go and have a bash at Miss Dawn Grey. She's a lovely piece of homework. I'll meet you after for a drink.

SIMON. You're sure you wouldn't . . . ?

TONY. Not at all, old man. You were here first . . . Off you go . . . (SIMON *disappears with the* S.M.) Salt of the earth, old Simon. Takes his work awfully serious, y'know. We studied medicine together at St. Swithin's—lovely, wasted years. Just think of it—we sweated blood over those exams.—and for what? When you're in general practice in Mayfair you don't need all that rigmarole. You can diagnose half your patients as soon as you step through the front door, with a bit of practice: brass gongs on the wall and tiger skins on the floor mean high blood pressure, box of chocolates on the piano and a pekinese on the mat—that's obesity; bills on the hall table and cigar ash on the carpet—there's a duodenal ulcer upstairs. It's as simple as that really. You don't need to see the curate's legs sticking out from under the bed to spot a case of female frustration You see? I've been working with a broken thermometer for two years—the only thing I use it for is to shut the patient up. Still, I was telling you about old Simon. When he first came to St. Swithins he smelt of Lifebouy soap and looked like a refugee from an orphanage. The one thought in his nut was how to

ACT I   DOCTOR IN THE HOUSE   11

become a doctor. Still is, come to that. Our problem was how to scale him down a bit, make his better self come to the surface. Good chap fundamentally, you see—but he needed humanizing. He turned up one evening just before term started . . looking a bit like a startled stag at sundown . . . John Evans was studying hard . . . as usual . . . (*He goes through the tabs. After a moment the curtain rises on Act I, Scene 1.*)

ACT ONE

Scene 1

The sitting-room of the flat. Books everywhere· on the floor, on the table, under furniture; in one corner a microscope on a stand, in another an old and battered piano. From the top of the piano a skull grins down on the room· the skull is wearing an old green hat with a white cord around it. Two or three battered armchairs of varying styles, and a large and equally battered couch. There are also many items of sportsgear lying around rugger boots, coloured socks, a couple of cricket bats, a dartbord on a splintered plywood backing. And there is a collection of signs, notices, and minor pieces of civic decoration a thirty m.p.h. sign, an orange beacon, a policeman's helmet, a "Gents" sign, an opening-and-closing sign from a park, and a notice prohibiting the passing of betting slips, a bus-stop and a couple of foreign signs Stage L *, there are windows overlooking the street. Stage* R., *a door leading to hall, this door is open.* U. S. *two doors—the one on the right leading to the kitchen and* GRIMSDYKE'S *bedroom; the other to* EVANS' *bedroom and the bathroom.*

At rise, JOHN EVANS *is discovered standing* R. *of the table finishing washing a rugger shirt in a zinc bowl. He wrings it out and carries it and the bowl of water to the* D S. *window, which is open, and pours the contents outside. There is an angry "Hey!" from a passer-by. From the direction of the right bedroom there comes a furious banging of drawers, and voices raised in argument. They are the voices of* TONY GRIMSDYKE *and his girl-friend,* VERA. JOHN EVANS *ignores the noise as he puts the empty bowl on the window-seat* D. S. *and goes up to a clothes line which is tied between the* U. S. *window and the door-jamb* U. L. *He hangs the shirt over this. All this while he is smoking a pipe and humming to himself. He stops humming and crosses to the chair* R. *of table and sits with his feet up on the table. Picks up a copy of* The Sporting Life *from the table and reads, paying no attention to the noise going on around him.*

TONY. (*Off.*) Socks, socks, socks! That's not much to ask for . . . I ought to have hundreds . . .

VERA. (*Off.*) Well, don't blame me . . . I don't hide your socks . . .

TONY. (*Coming in to behind armchair* D. R. *and looking under the cushion.*) I'm always buying socks. I spend a fortune on socks . . . what have you done with 'em all? (*To the piano* C. B. *He lifts the keyboard lid knocking out some music and a newspaper which are there.*)

(*We now see that* TONY, *as he hurries round the room looking everywhere for socks, has one sock on and one bare foot.* VERA *comes in from bedroom slamming the door after her. She stands above the* R. *end of sofa, talking to* TONY *who is now searching under the sofa cushions where he finds nothing but old newspapers.*)

VERA. (*A very beautiful girl, speaks with a slight accent.*) What have *I* done with them! Listen to him. You think I want your socks? You think I eat them?

TONY. (*Stops searching and faces her across the sofa.*)

I wouldn't put that past you! Out of spite—just to gratify your blasted temper—you'd be quite capable of boiling my socks and eating them with white sauce! (TONY *searches again in the sofa.* VERA *comes to below* R. *end of sofa.*)

VERA. I don't like white sauce! Just because you've lost one sock—is that the end of the world?

TONY. (*Crosses to* L. *below the table.*) One sock! O ye gods. Not one sock, Vera, my dear, dotty, dimwit. (*Turns to face her and crosses back to* C.) Hundreds of socks. Mountains of 'em—dwindled away until all I have is this!

(*During this spiel,* SIMON SPARROW *enters* D. R. *He has a large canvas hold-all, a copy of Gray's* Anatomy *under one arm, and he stands diffidently in the entrance. As the scene progresses he shifts the heavy volume from one arm to the other and drops his bag.*)

VERA. (*Icily.*) A man with your talent for exaggeration should be in commercial TV.

TONY. Don't change the subject, woman. (*To behind* JOHN'S *back.*) John—have you got any socks?

JOHN. (*Without looking up from his paper.*) No.

TONY. Liar. Let's look . . . (*Tries to grab* JOHN'S *foot.* JOHN *quickly puts feet on the floor.*)

VERA. (*Pulls* TONY *away from* JOHN.) Don't let him, Johnnie. If he wants socks he should buy them.

TONY. Buy them! Didn't I buy socks only last week?

VERA. No.

TONY. (*To behind* JOHN, *putting hand on his shoulder.*) John—be a sport. I need socks. One sock . . .

SIMON. Er . . . hello . . .

TONY. Hello (*Speaks over his shoulder, turning straight back to* JOHN.) Haven't you got any spares?

JOHN. Nope.

SIMON. (*Clearing his throat.*) I was told . . .

TONY. (*Crossing to below* R. *of sofa. To* SIMON.) Look, old boy, do you happen to have any socks?

SIMON. Why, yes, I have . . .

TONY. Where are they?

SIMON. Well . . . I've got one pair on . . . and a couple pairs in my bag . . .

TONY. The man's rolling in socks. I'm Tony Grimsdyke . . . (*Shakes hands with* SIMON.) pleased to know you . . .

SIMON. I'm Simon Sparrow . . .

TONY. You can't help that . . . Listen . . . (*Taking* SIMON *a step or two* R) will you lend me a pair of socks until tomorrow?

VERA. (*Crossing to* TONY'S L.) Say "no."

SIMON (*A little bewildered.*) Yes . . . (VERA.) No?

VERA (*Backing a pace* L.) You'll never get 'em back. He ruins socks.

TONY. (*Right up to* VERA.) Shut up!

VERA. Don't shout at me!

TONY I'm wanting the socks—not you!

VERA. (*Walks towards armchair* D. C. *making* TONY *back, facing her all the time.*) If you shout at me again, like that, I will walk out of this flat and never come back! (JOHN *"comes to," realizes what is being said*)

TONY. Good!

VERA. Right! (*She turns and strides up to the door* U. R. JOHN *puts his paper down on the table and hurries across to stop her in the doorway.*) Moi, je peux pas vivre avec un type comme ça . . .

(TONY *makes a move after her and stubs his toe painfully on the corner of the armchair. He stands below the drinks cabinet rubbing his toe, facing* D. S. *She smiles at this.* JOHN *stops her.*)

JOHN. Oh no—Vera . . . not again.

VERA. Again what?

JOHN. Don't walk out again. When you walked out for

ACT I DOCTOR IN THE HOUSE 15

good the day before yesterday we had haricot beans for supper.

VERA. It will make you appreciate me.

JOHN. Tony, stop her . . .

TONY. (*Stops rubbing toe but doesn't face the others.*) Let her go.

JOHN. (*Crossing to behind* TONY, *putting both hands on* TONY'S *shoulders.*) Your memory is too short. Don't you *remember* those beans—yellow, indigestible, gaseous . . . (VERA *opens the door.* JOHN *turns up to her*) Vera —don't go. Tony is sorry . . . (*Looking hard at* TONY, *to make him apologize.*)

VERA. (*Looking at* TONY.) Is he?

TONY. Oh! . . . (*Turns to face* VERA. *Shouts.*) Yes, I'm sorry.

VERA. You don't sound it.

TONY. (*Facing front.*) It'll take more than a plateful of haricot beans to make me crawl.

VERA. Well!

JOHN. Tony . . .

VERA I *was* making ravioli for supper.

JOHN.
TONY. } (*Together as they both face* VERA.) { Ravioli!
Ravioli!

VERA. (*Turns as if to go.*) But in the circumstances . . .

(*Crossing* JOHN, TONY *goes up to* R. *of* VERA, *puts arm round her shoulder and brings her down on his* L. *to between sofa and armchair.* JOHN *starts to cross* L.)

TONY. Vera, old girl, I 'umbly apologize. I don't care if you did lose my socks.

VERA. I did not lose your socks! (*She turns and starts to go angrily* U. S.)

JOHN. (*Crossing down to* VERA *and pushing* VERA *back to face* TONY *again, profile to audience.*) Tony! For heaven's sake . . .

TONY. I mean—I don't care about socks. After all—a

man can learn to forget socks. For me—they shall be a thing of the past—an echo.

JOHN. (*Crosses behind sofa to table, picks up his paper.*) The brave music of a distant drum.

TONY. What's the plural of ravioli?

JOHN. Raviolis? (*Crosses to sofa. Sits U. S. end with his feet up, reads paper again.*)

TONY. (*Kissing* VERA) Who cares? Yum . . . my songbird, my dove, my chickadee . . .

SIMON. (*Tentatively.*) Did you want to borrow any socks?

TONY. (*Absorbed.*) Tell the man to go away, darling.

VERA. Go away . . . (*She kisses* TONY.)

SIMON. But . . .

TONY. Go away!

SIMON. I was told to come here; you see . . . My name is Sparrow . . . Simon Sparrow . . . my uncle . . . (*His voice dies away.*)

TONY. (*Reluctantly stops kissing* VERA.) Later, old girl. The mood is right, but the moment is wrong. (*Takes* VERA *to armchair* D. C., *puts her in it. Then crosses to below* R. *end of sofa.*) The name Sparrow rings a bell . . .

SIMON. (*Crosses to* TONY'S R) I've come to join the medical school at St. Swithin's and I was told that . . .

JOHN. You're a new student? (JOHN *kneels up on* D. S. *end of sofa, puts his paper behind sofa cushion.* VERA *sits up straight also looking* SIMON *up and down.*)

SIMON. Yes . . .

(*They survey him in silence for a moment or two.* TONY *walks round him in a complete clockwise circle ending* L. *of him again.*)

TONY. This, gentlemen, is a rare and great occasion. We are in the presence of royal blood In the veins of this handsome example of the species man runs the true blood of Sir Lancelot Spatt!

JOHN. (*Crosses a pace* D. L. *to pouffe.*) Old Blood-and-Thunder's nephew, by gosh.

SIMON. That's right . . .
TONY. Crikey!
SIMON. I *can* lend you some socks, if you like.
VERA. You are really the nephew of Sir Lancelot?
SIMON Yes. I am Though I'm afraid I don't know him awfully well. (*Crosses below* TONY *to between him and* JOHN, *addressing* JOHN *now.*) My father is a doctor, you see, and he wrote to Sir Lancelot and asked him to get me into St. Swithin's.
TONY What for?
SIMON. (*Faintly surprised. Turning to face* TONY.) I mean—into the Medical School.
TONY. I realize that, old boy. (*Closing in on* SIMON'S R. *while* JOHN *does the same on his* L.) What I want to know is why you want to get into Medical School.
SIMON. I thought I'd like to become a doctor.
TONY. What for?
SIMON. Well . . .
VERA. (*Rises, crosses to* TONY'S R., *pulls him away a little and stands slightly behind his* R. *shoulder.*) Stop teasing him, Tony. He means it. He's not like you. Some people think it is a good profession.
TONY. It takes all kinds to make a world, I suppose. So your uncle got you in?
SIMON. I . . . I don't know. He just sent a wire to Father telling me to come along. His secretary told me to come to this address.
TONY. You're very welcome, old chap. This is John Evans . . . (SIMON *turns to* JOHN *who says* "How do you do?" *and shakes hands.*) and this is Vera. (SIMON *turns to face* VERA *who says* "Hello" *and shakes hands, while* TONY *crosses* R *and picks up* SIMON'S *bag and takes it to below the divan, saying* "Oh" *as he lifts it and feels how heavy it is.*) I'm Tony Grimsdyke—or did I tell you that?

(SIMON *crosses* VERA, *who takes the book out of his* L. *hand while* JOHN *takes the raincoat off his* R. *arm as he goes He goes up behind the armchair level with* TONY, *who is by the* D. S. *end of the divan. Meanwhile* VERA *takes the book and puts it on the sofa table, standing at the* D. S. *end of it, and* JOHN *has taken his coat and hung it on the door* U. L.)

SIMON. Yes . . . but it doesn't matter. My name is Simon.

TONY. Old Blood-and . . . (*Drops the bag with a loud thud at the foot of the divan.* SIMON *looks concerned but says nothing.*) I mean, your uncle, spoke to me about you. Asked me to give you a bed for the night.

SIMON. Jolly decent of you—but I don't want to intrude.

TONY. A pleasure. (*Sits* SIMON *in the armchair and stands behind it, on the* L. *side.* JOHN *picks up the things that* TONY *swept off the keyboard and puts them under the cushion of the piano stool. Then stands beside it.*) Self-interest, old boy. I want to keep on the right side of his nibs. You may not know it, Simon, but your uncle is the lord of St. Swithin's.

SIMON. I gathered he was pretty high-up. But he's never had much to do with the family.

JOHN. High up! (*Comes down and sits on pouffe, facing* SIMON.) What Sir Lancelot says goes. If it doesn't he regards it as a personal affront.

SIMON. What is he like?

VERA. (*Comes round the* D. S. *corner of sofa and sits on arm.*) Haven't you seen him?

SIMON. Only from photographs.

TONY. I would describe him as a cross between a Barbary slave-master with chronic indigestion . . .

JOHN. And an African gorilla with an irritating skin disease.

TONY. No disrespect intended to your relatives, Simon.

SIMON. None taken. Is he a good surgeon?

TONY. Well . . . John, what would you say?

SIMON. I mean, he's awfully famous and all that. A knighthood—you don't get that for nothing.

TONY. For nothing! (*Crosses to above sofa.*) Good grief, he had to pay through the nose.

JOHN. What really got him started was his cure for rheumatism.

SIMON. He made a reputation for that, didn't he?

TONY. More than a reputation, old boy. (*Crosses to R. of table L.*) He also made a house in Harley Street, a cottage in Sussex, a yacht, a Rolls, and (*Sits on R. edge of table.*) similar sordid perks.

SIMON. What was the cure exactly?

JOHN. Well most people over the age of fifty have rheumatism of one sort or another. Old Blood-and-Thunder used to cut 'em up and remove all the organs not strictly necessary for the continuance of life.

SIMON. Did it make them better?

TONY. It didn't make 'em worse (*Rises. Crosses up to piano, taking out a cigarette and gets a match from R. end of piano top.*) and your uncle was able to persuade them they felt better. I tell you his practice increased ten-fold overnight (*Lights cigarette and flicks match into the air.*)

JOHN. He's never looked back since. Calls himself the last of the general surgeons. None of this specialization for him.

SIMON. A "general" surgeon?

TONY. (*Crosses to* SIMON. *Stays L. of armchair.*) What you'd call an all-rounder. He claims he can remove your stomach, take out your tonsils, cut off a leg or whip out a lung with equal dexterity.

SIMON. But he's very successful.

TONY. He has a fair average. Fifty per cent success, fifty per cent funerals.

JOHN. I'll give him this, though—he can carve a turkey. You should see him at Christmas—he whistles through it! Slices thin as wafers, and not a bit of meat left on the bone. Puts you off your dinner watching him.

VERA. (*Rises. Gestures to* JOHN *to stop, turns* R *to* TONY.) That's enough, Johnnie. Tony, give Simon a drink.

TONY. Good show. Spot of Gunga, old boy?

SIMON. Gunga?

TONY. Gunga Din—gin.

SIMON. No thanks. (*Rises, facing* TONY.) Never touch it.

TONY. (*Incredulous.*) You don't? (TONY *and* JOHN *exchange looks.*)

JOHN. No?

SIMON. Beer occasionally.

TONY. Oh . . . You had me worried for a moment. John, have we got any wallop?

JOHN. (*Staring to rise.*) Sure . . .

VERA. I'll get some. (*She goes off* U. R., *smiling at* SIMON.)

SIMON. (*He steps in a pace* L.) Is . . . er . . . she a medical student?

(JOHN *laughs.*)

TONY. Lord, no. (*Comes in front of sofa, puts a cushion against* U. S. *arm, sits with feet up, and head resting on cushion.*) She's a . . . a . . . John, what is Vera?

JOHN. (*Rises and crosses a step* U. S. *to* TONY.) Well —er—she . . . more or less runs the show for us. D'you see? (*Drifts* L. *towards the table.*)

SIMON. Lives here?

TONY. More or less. She has the room above this— and spends her time doing for us.

SIMON. (*To cover the implication of* TONY's *reply, takes a step away* R., *turns back to* TONY, *changing the subject.*) I suppose you've been at St. Swithin's some time?

TONY. Four years.

SIMON. You've nearly finished your course then?

(TONY *and* JOHN *both roar with laughter.*)

JOHN. (*Sits on the* R. *edge of table, his feet on the chair.*) Not him!

SIMON. But surely if he has four years' study to his credit . . .

TONY. Ah, the ingenuousness of youth! Exams, old boy, exams—they're the thing. I've come down in my anatomy four times now.

SIMON. Failed?

TONY. Failed. I'm not a minute senior to you. And at the end of term I shall fail again—with reasonable luck.

(*Pause.*)

SIMON. I see. (*He says "I see" being completely mystified, and crosses to the armchair and sits on the* L *arm.*)

TONY. You don't really—but let it ride. Above all, don't waste sympathy on me, old boy. (*Sits up in the sofa, his feet still up*) All my failures were achieved with careful forethought.

SIMON. You fail on *purpose?* Why?

JOHN. (*Gets off the table. Crosses above the sofa, stands below sofa table on* SIMON's L) It's quite simple, old chap. Tony's grandmother made a will in which she left him a thousand a year for as long as he was a medical student.

TONY. Her one wish was that I should be a medical gentleman. Dear old soul. She put the clause in her will in case she should pop off while I was in the middle of the course. Her faith in doctors was misplaced. Soon after she made the will she was called to that bourne from which no traveller returns . . .

JOHN. And so Tony found himself with a nice little income providing he remained a medical student. (*Sits on* D. S. *corner of sofa table.*)

SIMON. I'm beginning to see.

TONY. Don't see any reason why I shouldn't carry on indefinitely. There's no law which says a man can't be a medical student at fifty—sixty . . . I flatter myself, old boy, that I have discovered the secret of gracious living. Oh, yes, the old legacy is good for a few more years yet!

VERA (*Entering from* U. R. *with a quart bottle of beer and a glass.*) That's what you think. (*Comes down to behind* U. S *end of sofa, leans over to* TONY.)

JOHN. (*Rises and turns to face* VERA.) Uh-uh! The fly in the ointment.

VERA. I will not marry an old medical student with whiskers. (*Crosses to above table* L, *puts down the glass and bottle of beer.*) Pass your exams this term, my boy, or out I go.

TONY. Did I mention marriage?

JOHN. No.

TONY. Did *you* mention marriage?

JOHN. No.

TONY. Then who brought up the blessed subject?

VERA. I did. (*She unscrews the stopper from the beer bottle.*)

TONY. I might have known it. (*Rises. Crosses to piano, stubs out cigarette in ash tray, gets three glasses from top of piano and takes them to top of table on* VERA'S R, *where he pours out four glasses of beer.*)

JOHN. (*Moves down and sits on* D. S. *arm of sofa.*) She's been reading Aldous Huxley again.

VERA. This term you get down to work, Tony. And you, too, John.

SIMON. (*To* JOHN.) You're not in the same boat as Grimsdyke?

JOHN. (*Rises, pats* SIMON'S *shoulder indicating "come along."* SIMON *rises and follows* JOHN *to* D. S R. *of table.*) Good lord, no! I haven't any grandmothers with money in the mattresses. Mine haven't got any mattresses. No, I've just passed in anatomy! I'm on my way to becoming a real doctor. I've even got a stethoscope (*Picks up stethoscope from table, and turns half* R *facing* SIMON.)

TONY. Don't let it go to your head, sonnie.

JOHN. I only just scraped through the exams. (*Puts

ACT I   DOCTOR IN THE HOUSE   23

stethoscope round his neck.) Didn't put in enough time at the lectures.
  TONY. Rugger. A rugger fiend.
  JOHN. I say, do you play?
  SIMON. A bit.
  JOHN. Oh, jolly good! We've got a . . .

(SIMON *crosses in front of* JOHN, *below table to* L. *of it.* TONY *hands him a glass of beer. Then gives one to* VERA, *one to* JOHN *and takes his own.* JOHN *puts chair* R. *of table in under table.*)

  SIMON. Yes, but if I get admitted to St. Swithin's I'll have to work. My folks can't afford to stretch it. I'll have to pass first crack.
  TONY. Get admitted? And old Blood-and-Thunder's your uncle? There ain't a doubt, old boy. We'll drink to it. We'll drink to him. (*They raise their glasses.*) To Sir Lancelot Spatt, better known as Blood-and-Thunder, the best butcher this side of Smithfield—may his discs never slip!
  SIR LANCELOT. (*Off—in a roar.*) Anyone home?

(*They all look anxiously towards the door* D. R. *They end their drinking abruptly as* SIR LANCELOT *himself appears. He is bearded, energetic, completely self-centred, a terrific bulldozer of a man.*)

  TONY. Crikey! Talk of the devil . . . Good evening, sir. Welcome to our little—er—home.

(SIR LANCELOT *enters a few paces, stands surveying the room.* TONY *puts down his glass on the table and hurries* D. R *to meet* SIR LANCELOT. JOHN *crosses to* L. *of* U. S. *arm of sofa, still holding his glass.* VERA *leaves her glass on the table and stands just* R. *of it.*)

  SIR LANCELOT. (*Looking round.*) Home? Home? Looks

like the lost-property office at Euston. Now, which one of you is my nephew, eh? (*To* TONY.) Not you, I hope. (*Pushes* TONY *out of the way with his stick. Crosses up to* L. *of* JOHN.) You? No, your face is too familiar. (*Crosses* JOHN, *sees* VERA.) Oh, dear, no! (*Turns away* D. S. *to* D. S. R. *edge of table*)

SIMON. (*Stepping down level with* SIR LANCELOT *to below* L. *corner of table*.) I am, sir.

SIR LANCELOT. (*A step towards* SIMON.) Oh, you are, eh? Bit skinny, aren't you? Have to put on more weight if you're going to be a surgeon. Very important to have a stomach in surgery. Gives the patient confidence.

(VERA *crosses to above armchair* R.)

SIMON. I hope to be a G. P., sir.

SIR LANCELOT. You'll be what I tell you to be. Hm— got your mother's looks. How is she?

(JOHN *goes up to piano, puts his glass of beer on piano top, takes off his stethoscope, puts it down on piano top, then crosses to* R. *of table*)

SIMON. Well . . .

SIR LANCELOT. (*Cutting in.*) Oh, don't tell me. I can't do anything for her. Too damn busy. Well, you're a blasted nuisance, boy. Still we'll do what we can for you. (*Crosses* R. *to* D. S. *end of sofa facing* TONY.) He can stay here?

TONY. For the night, sir, yes.

SIR LANCELOT. For the night? For the duration, boy. I can't have him hopping all over the place like a blasted bird I'm responsible for him.

JOHN. (*Crosses down to* SIR LANCELOT'S L.) We'd love to have him, sir, but we haven't the room.

SIR LANCELOT. (*Turns to face* JOHN) No room? Nonsense! The place is like a hotel (*Turning towards* TONY *and looking up at door* U. R.) How many bedrooms are there?

JOHN. Only two, sir.

SIR LANCELOT. (*Pointing with his stick to door* U. R.) Who sleeps in that one?

TONY. I do, sir.

SIR LANCELOT. And this one? (*Striding to door* U. L.)

JOHN. (*Quickly following him.*) Er—mine, sir.

SIR LANCELOT. (*Opening the door.*) Enormous! (*He slams the door and turns round to face* JOHN *who is on his* R.) On your own?

JOHN. I take up an awful lot of room, sir.

SIR LANCELOT. That's settled, then. Simon stays here with you. (*Crosses down to top* R. *edge of table.*) That's your room, boy. (*Crosses to* TONY'S L.) Make your terms with these gentlemen, and don't let 'em twist you. (JOHN *crosses down to* U. R. *corner of table*)

SIMON. (*Crossing below table to* D. C.) I don't think I'd better.

SIR LANCELOT. (*Turning to face* SIMON.) Speak up, boy. Don't mutter. You don't think what . . . ?

SIMON. That I ought to force myself on these people. They've already been very kind offering me a bed for tonight and . . .

VERA. (*Crossing down to* R. *of* TONY *just behind his shoulder.*) We'd like to have you, Simon. Wouldn't we, Tony?

TONY. (*Half heartedly.*) Yes— (VERA *nudges him violently, he turns his head quickly to face* SIR LANCELOT *and says the second "yes" very enthusiatically.*) oh, yes!

SIMON. But I haven't even been accepted by the Medical School yet. Haven't had an interview . . .

SIR LANCELOT. Accepted? Accepted? (*Turns to face* TONY.) What's the boy drivelling on about now?

SIMON. (*Crosses to below table, turns to face* SIR LANCELOT.) I've got an interview with the Dean. He'll want to ask me questions—find out whether I'll make a good doctor . . . er . . . won't he?

SIR LANCELOT. Make a good doctor? You must be weak in the head, boy. (*Crosses to bottom* R. *corner of table.* JOHN *crosses to sofa, sits* U. S. *arm.*) I'll tell you exactly what he'll ask you . . . Have you been to a public school?

SIMON. Yes.

(TONY *sits* D. S. *arm of sofa.* VERA *stands behind him.*)

SIR LANCELOT. Your people can afford the fees and that sort of thing?

SIMON. Well . . .

SIR LANCELOT. That goes without saying. You play football, of course?

SIMON. Yes, sir . . .

SIR LANCELOT. Which kind? Watch it—it's very important . . .

SIMON. Rugger, sir. (JOHN *and* TONY *exchange pleased looks.*)

SIR LANCELOT. Good. Which position?

SIMON. Wing three-quarter.

JOHN. (*Delighted. He rises, takes a step towards* SIMON.) Three-quarter, eh?

SIR LANCELOT. (*Thunderous, turns to face* JOHN, *bangs with his stick on floor.* JOHN *sits again on sofa arm, abashed.*) First fifteen at school?

SIMON. Oh, yes, sir.

SIR LANCELOT. Mmm, pity you're so skinny, still I suppose you've got the speed?

SIMON. I've got cups for the hundred.

SIR LANCELOT Well, you may shape well. Lucky you're a three. The blessed hospital's full of forwards. Welcome to St. Swithin's, boy, (*Shakes* SIMON's *hand.*) much pleasure in accepting you.

SIMON. (*After a surprised pause.*) Is that all, sir?

SIR LANCELOT. Well, the interview hasn't varied, except for the odd word here and there, in twenty-five years. Good day to you, my boy. Don't bother me unless you have to. You may make a surgeon in time—just develop your powers. (*Crosses in front of them all to*

ACT I   DOCTOR IN THE HOUSE   27

below armchair D. R. *As he moves, all rise,* JOHN D. S *a pace. All three boys have both hands in trousers pockets.*) A successful surgeon must have the eye of a hawk, the heart of a lion and the hand of a lady. (*Turns to face them*) And don't let me catch you slopping about my hospital with your hands in your pockets. (*To* SIMON.) You! (SIMON *takes hands out of pockets.* TONY *turns L. looking at* SIMON *To* JOHN.) You! (JOHN *takes his hands out of pockets Hitting* TONY'S *behind with his cane.*) Come on! (TONY *turns quickly to face* SIR LANCE- LOT *taking his hands out of pockets.*) It's all very well for errand boys, but you're supposed to be medical students. Besides which, the habit can lead to osteo- arthritis of the shoulder girdle in middle age. So watch it. Stand up straight. (*All three boys stand to attention.*) And you, Grimsdyke, (TONY *takes a "military" pace to- wards* SIR LANCELOT.) if you intend to frequent my school this term, buy another sock! (TONY, *standing on his* L *leg, puts* R *foot behind* L. *calf.*) Good day, gentle- men. (*He sweeps out.*)

CURTAIN

SCENE 2

The flat a few days later. The curtains of both windows are closed. The standard lamp L. *of the piano, the small lamp on the corner cupboard* U. L., *and the light* U. R. *are all lit.*

SIMON *is discovered sitting in the chair above table, studing Gray's* Anatomy. VERA *enters from bed- room,* U. R., *humming to herself She is wearing a skirt but her top part is bare except for the brassière which she is holding in place with her hands. She is also carrying a blouse as she crosses above the sofa, leaving her blouse on the* U. S. *arm and goes to* SIMON'S L. *She proffers her back to him.*

VERA. Simon—fasten this for me, will you?
SIMON. (*Not looking up from his book.*) Hum?
VERA. My thingmebob. (*She backs right into him.*)
SIMON. (*Comes back to reality with a start. He is rather embarrassed.*) Oh, yes . . . (*He fumbles with the fastening at the back.*)
VERA. Take your time . . .
SIMON. It's rather awkward— (*He rises, struggling with the fastener.*) the fastener is bent . . .
VERA. That's always happening . . . (*She starts to cross to the sofa pulling him after her.*)
SIMON Wait.
VERA. Sorry. (*She stops* L. *of the sofa.*)
SIMON. And—it is—rather—tight . . .
VERA. Gives me uplift . . .
SIMON. Hm? Oh, yes . . . there . . . it's done . . .
VERA. (*Turning, smiling*) Thank you, dear Simon . . .
SIMON. (*Backing a little*) Not at all.
VERA. Do I make you embarrassed, yes?
SIMON. Yes . . . I mean . . . No . . . (*He turns front.*)
VERA. I mean—it's good practice for you after all, isn't that so?
SIMON. I don't actually wear those things myself.
VERA. Ooh, ooh! I've got a rather awful stiffness in my knee. I wonder if you'd look at it for me?
SIMON. (*Really embarrassed.*) Your knee?
VERA. This one. (*Puts her* R. *foot on pouffe, lifts skirt and points at knee.*) Just here . . .
SIMON. (*Edges towards her, tentatively stretches out his* L *hand, but just before it reaches her knee, he withdraws it and recoils* R. *to* R. *corner of sofa*) I really don't think I'm qualified, you know . . .
VERA. (*Straightens up, drops her leg, laughs.*) Poor Simon. It isn't right to tease you like this. I don't mean it.

SIMON. Your knee is all right?
VERA. Don't you think so?
SIMON. (*He smiles and crosses to her.*) Oh yes. It's a jolly good knee . . . (*She quickly puts leg up on pouffe and reveals her knee again. He hurriedly retreats R. She laughs.*) Well, I mean . . .

VERA. (*Goes to U. S. sofa arm, picks up her blouse and puts it on, standing above sofa arm.* SIMON *stands below* D. S. *sofa arm facing* D. S.) Don't worry. You're very sweet really, Simon. And so serious. You put the others to shame.

SIMON. I can't afford to flunk the exams. Dad's a bit pushed for cash, you know, and this course is really costing him more than he can afford. I mustn't let him down.

VERA. But your uncle—Sir Lancelot—Tony says he's —what does he say?—bloody stinking rich.

SIMON. I couldn't take anything from him. (*Sits on* D. S *arm of sofa.*) No . . . I've got to do this under my own steam—and I mustn't take a day longer than necessary, or there won't be any money in the kitty.

VERA. (*Comes round sofa arm to* C. *front of sofa, adjusts suspenders of* L. *stocking.*) You will make a good doctor, I think.

SIMON. I wish I thought so.

VERA. You believe in it, don't you? I mean—you think being a doctor is something special and important.

SIMON. I suppose I do.

VERA. Tony—and even John—they're so cynical. To them everything is a joke. (*Sits next to* SIMON *on* D. S. *end of sofa.*) Don't let them make you that way, Simon.

SIMON. They don't really mean it. Besides, there is some truth in it, I suppose. But there's another side to it as well. I've watched my father—he's not a wonderful doctor, by any means—but—I don't know—every so often he does something which, well, seems to make up for all the odd bits of quackery.

VERA. I know what you mean—my father was a doctor, too, in Paris.

SIMON. Oh, I'm sorry . . .

VERA. Sorry?

SIMON. You said he *was* a doctor. I thought . . .

VERA. Oh, he's only dead medically speaking. He got too friendly with a woman patient. (SIMON *laughs.*) Poor Daddy! (*There is a knock at the door.*) Who's that? (*She rises. The door opens to admit* BROMLEY, *a porter at the hospital. He is a wry little cockney of about fifty.*) Ah, Bromley. (*Crosses in front of* SIMON *to* R. *of sofa.* BROMLEY *comes to below armchair.*) Come in.

BROMLEY. Well I really came to see Mr. Sprarow, miss. Not that you aren't always a sight for sore eyes.

VERA. Bromley has such natural good manners, Simon. He makes me feel ashamed of Tony.

BROMLEY. You can't blame Mr. Grimsdyke, miss. He went to one of these pukka schools. Nothing like a pukka school for learning you real shocking manners!

SIMON. (*Rises, crossing to face* BROMLEY.) Did you get it, Bromley?

(VERA *moves round* D. S. *corner of sofa and sits on* D. S. *arm.*)

BROMLEY. Not "it," Mr. Sparrow, sir. "Him." Charley would be downright offended if he heard you calling him an "it."

SIMON. I beg Charley's pardon.

BROMLEY. I've got him outside now, sir. You want him in?

SIMON. Please.

BROMLEY. (*Throws hat into armchair Crosses to door, opens it.* SIMON *follows to door and holds it open.*) Thought I'd better see the lay of the land first, y'see. Not everyone takes to Charley at first sight. (*He goes out of the door, and returns at once carrying a skeleton by hook in the skull, crosses* SIMON *to* R. *of* VERA. SIMON *closes door, comes in to below armchair.*) Here he is in all his glory—Charley. Charley, meet Mr. Sparrow. (*He holds out* CHARLEY'S *hand which* SIMON *shakes.*) And Miss Vera. (*He makes* CHARLEY *bow to* VERA.) Got a nice head, ain't he, sir? There's real character there. (*Indicating the divan* U. R.) Over here, sir?

SIMON. Yes. Thanks, Bromley. (BROMLEY *takes skeleton to divan and places him full length, his skull on the cushions at* U. S. *end.* SIMON *follows him up and stands* L. *of him.*) Was it—I mean he—what you said?

BROMLEY. 'fraid not, sir. Had to pay a dollar over the odds. Can't pick up Charleys like you used to be able to.

SIMON. (*Feels in his trousers pockets.*) Er . . . I'll settle later.

BROMLEY. No hurry, sir. (*Takes out a handkerchief and mops his brow.*) I was just wondering though—could I have a drink of water? Charley's bit of a handful—I sweated out a lot of moisture.

SIMON. (*Crosses to in front of piano.*) Sure. I'll get you one.

BROMLEY. (*Disappointed.*) You will, sir? (*Eyeing the quart bottle of beer on the drinks cabinet rather pointedly.* SIMON *turns to face him as he speaks. Notes* BROMLEY'S *hint.*) Much obliged, I'm sure.

SIMON. Unless you'd rather have a glass of beer?

BROMLEY. (*Up to* SIMON'S R.) Now you mention it, sir, a glass of beer would go down very well . . .

VERA. (*Rises, crosses up to drinks cabinet* U. R., *where she takes the bottle and pours out two glasses of beer—the glasses are also on the cupboard top.*) All right—I'll get it. You too, Simon?

SIMON. (*Returns to top of table, sits and looks at his book.*) Please . . .

BROMLEY. (*Crosses to* SIMON'S R. *at table.*) Hard at it I see, sir.

SIMON. Making a start, Bromley.

BROMLEY. (*Pointing to* SIMON'S *book.*) You got Gray's *Anatomy* there, I see.

SIMON. You know it?

BROMLEY. Bless you, sir, I know it backwards. (*A step* R.) Got one at home, you know. Keeps the kids quiet on wet days. They love looking at all them lovely coloured drawings—yellow nerves, lovely red arteries, brown bladders, long blue veins, regular picnic it is.

(VERA *takes the two glasses of beer and crosses* L *to* BROMLEY'S R.)

SIMON. Yes, I see what you mean.

VERA. (*Handing* BROMLEY *a drink.*) *Voilà*, Bromley.

BROMLEY. Thank you, miss. (BROMLEY *takes glass.* VERA *crosses behind him to* SIMON *and gives* SIMON *his glass.*) Well, here's a health to our fraternity, Mr. Sparrow. (*Holds up glass to* SIMON. SIMON *takes small sip of his, puts glass down on* U. R. *corner of table. As* BROMLEY *knocks back his beer in one drink,* VERA *crosses* R. *behind him to his* R. *watching the operation, fascinated. As he finishes he turns to face* VERA) Aah . . .

VERA. More?

BROMLEY. (*Immediately hands her the empty glass which she takes to refill at the drinks cabinet* U. R.) Might as well take the other half, miss . . . Thank you . . . (*As she goes to get it* BROMLEY *turns back to face* SIMON.) It's a great pity, Mr. Sparrow, sir, that you didn't start medicine twenty years ago.

SIMON. Might have been rather difficult for me. I'm not sure I could walk at the time.

BROMLEY. Naturally not, sir, naturally not. (VERA *brings drink to* BROMLEY *then goes to sofa, sits* U. S. *end with her feet up.*) What I am getting at is that our profession ain't what it was. No, sir—not by a long chalk. (*Taking drink.*) Thank you, miss. Now look at the patients, Mr. Sparrow. In them days—patients knew their place. (*Takes a drink.*)

SIMON And now they don't, you mean?

BROMLEY. Not by half. In the days before the N.H.S.

—National Health, Mr. Sparrow—the patients relied on us. Blimey, we didn't mollycoddle them then. Out-patients had to be in the building and sitting on the benches by eight o'clock. Then we locked the doors—anyone coming late had to wait till next day. (*Takes another drink.*)

VERA. But some of the cases you locked out might have been serious.

BROMLEY. (*A couple of steps to* VERA—L. *of sofa.*) Most of them what was locked out was, miss. Only the healthy ones could get up early enough to get in.

SIMON. It's one method, I suppose.

BROMLEY. (*Back to* R. *of* SIMON.) And it worked all right. That way we got through the whole lot in no time at all. (*Puts his empty glass at the* D. R. *corner of the table.*) And I never had but one accident all the years I was doing it!

SIMON. A remarkable record.

BROMLEY. Thank you, sir.

VERA. What was the accident?

BROMLEY. (*A couple of steps to her,* R. *of sofa.*) I had a bit of a hangover, miss, and sent a bronchitis case up to surgery. Before I could put it right they'd cut him open and whipped out his appendix. (*Back again to* R. *of* SIMON) Still, it's an ill wind, they say. You know, that bloke never came back any more—his bronchitis cleared up like magic. (*With seeming unconsciousness he picks up* SIMON'S *beer and drains it.* SIMON *rises, puts out his hand towards the glass, as* BROMLEY *lowers it after drinking.* BROMLEY *looks at* SIMON, *then at the glass, then again at* SIMON.) Was that your'n, sir? Begging your pardon, I didn't notice . . .

SIMON (*Takes the glass and puts it down on the table*) Never mind.

BROMLEY. (*Crosses* L *to* VERA'S R. SIMON *comes to in front of* U. R. *corner of table.* BROMLEY *turns to face* SIMON.) Well, this won't get the baby ironed, as they say. Mr. Sparrow, sir, you are at the beginning of what I am positive will be a long and honourable career.

You've got the looks of a doctor, (*Lifts both of* SIMON'S *hands, looks at them, turns them over, lets them drop.*) the hands of a doctor, the voice of a doctor. And I'd like to say this, sir. If—*if*—I say, there is any little particle of information I can pass on to you out of the vast store of knowledge I have gathered over the years, then you have but to ask, Mr. Sparrow, and John Lister Bromley will be only too pleased and happy to oblige.

SIMON. Thank you, Bromley, I'm most grateful.

BROMLEY. Not at all, sir. And beggin' your pardons, (*Crosses in front of armchair* D. R.) sir and miss, for being so loquacious. (*Picks up hat off armchair, goes to open door, but it flies open in his face knocking him back against armchair. He picks himself up and goes up to divan, giving a pat to "Charley."*) It's the beer what does it—oils me epiglottis . . .

(TONY *enters* R., *wearing a scarf with college colours, crosses to behind* VERA. SIMON *sits above table again and continues his interrupted study of Gray's Anatomy.*)

TONY. Stand aside, old lad. You'll get nephritis standing in a draught. (*Kisses the top of* VERA'S *head over the sofa back.*)

JOHN. (*Enters* R. *Stops below armchair. He also wears a college scarf.*) Sparrow! There you are! Where were you?

VERA. Here studying, as he should be.

JOHN. Studying! Oh, no. (*Goes angrily off to his room* U. L., *leaving his bedroom door open and switching on the light.*)

TONY. (*Examining the empty bottle on the cabinet.*) Who's been at the beer?

BROMLEY. (*Crosses to* TONY'S R.) Beer, sir? Did you say beer? I am rather dry, Mr. Grimsdyke.

VERA. He's had three already, Tony . . . two of his own and one of Simon's.

BROMLEY. An accident, sir, . . . quite unpremeditated . . .

TONY. Scram, Bromley . . . you've had it . . . scram . . .

BROMLEY. (*Crosses to door*, D. R.) Scram it is, sir. (*Opens door.*) I was just telling Mr. Sparrow, that if at any time . . .

TONY. Beat it! (*Picks up book from sofa table.*)

(TONY *chucks the book at* BROMLEY *who ducks round the door and departs. The book hits the closed door. He crosses to divan, takes off his scarf, throws it on to divan, then down to door, picks up the book, goes to behind sofa, throws book on divan.* JOHN *switches off the light in his bedroom and strides down to* R. *of* SIMON *behind table.* SIMON *is studying, his head resting in both hands—elbows on the table.* JOHN *has left his scarf in bedroom.*)

JOHN. Now . . . we can deal with this renegade. Simon—you chump, (SIMON *looks up.*) what about the rugger trial this afternoon?

SIMON. Oh, that . . . (*Goes back to his book.*)

JOHN. Oh, that . . . (*Shouting, pulls* SIMON'S *arms down on to table.*) I said *rugger* trial . . .

SIMON. I heard you.

VERA. We all heard you. They probably heard you in Stepney.

JOHN. (*Crossing towards* VERA.) Vera, you don't realize . . .

SIMON. (*Rises, moves a step to* R. *of table.*) I'm sorry, John. Fact is, I've decided to give up rugger.

JOHN. (*To* TONY.) Did he say—give up rugger?

TONY. (*To* SIMON.) Careful, old lad. You're getting very near the bone. Every man has an idol. John goes for rugger. I prefer sex myself. (*Crosses to armchair* D. R., *sits in it with his feet over* L. *arm facing* L.)

JOHN. Shut up, Tony. This is serious. (*Turns to face*

SIMON.) Simon, you're one of the best prospects we've had in years. And you talk about ditching it?

SIMON. (*To above table again.*) I don't want to. But I've got to concentrate on getting through these damned exams. (*Picks up his book.*) If I flunk even one, I've had it— (*Sits again above table—reads.*)

JOHN. (*Crosses above sofa, round back of it.*) This is fantastic. Absolutely and incredibly fantastic. (*Sits on D. S. arm of sofa facing front.* VERA *moves up sofa to U. S. end sitting on L. arm, her feet on the seat.*)

(*There is a loud "cooey" from the door, and they turn.*)

TONY. (*Imitating* RIGGIE's *"cooey" on* "Riggie.") Riggie—enter!

(*A nurse—dressed in civvies—comes in. This is* RIGGIE *—an abbreviation for Rigor Mortis. She is not unattractive, but she has a simple, dumb manner.*)

RIGGIE. (*Closes door behind her, marches over to* JOHN's R.) You were supposed to meet me at the Odeon.
JOHN. I was?
RIGGIE. Was it you?
JOHN. (*Rises.*) It certainly wasn't. I had a rugger trial.
RIGGIE. Then it was someone else. (*Moves round him to sofa arm, sits.*) Doesn't matter. I'm hungry.
JOHN. (*Turns to her.*) I say, Riggie, you can't stay here. Supposing Matron is on the snoop.
TONY. Entertaining of nurses in digs is stictly taboo, Simon. A deadly sin, punishable by slow death.
RIGGIE. Well, I *am* hungry. (*Crosses L. to* SIMON, *stands R. of table.* SIMON *rises, comes to corner of table, smiling at* RIGGIE.) Hello.
TONY. (*Rises, moves a step D. S.*) My dear Riggie, my apologies. (JOHN *sits D. S sofa arm.*) Simon, allow me to introduce to you a fellow worker in medicine. A nurse.

Affectionately known as Rigor Mortis. We call her Riggie.

RIGGIE. (*Giggling.*) Silly, isn't it?

TONY. And this is Simon Sparrow, a man born to be a consultant.

SIMON. How do you do? (SIMON *and* RIGGIE *shake hands.*)

RIGGIE. Have you anything to eat?

VERA. We were just going out to get something.

TONY. (*Crosses U. L. Stands above and between* SIMON *and* RIGGIE.) A better idea. Simon, old lad, you need to stretch your legs. On the corner—just below us—is a fish and chip shop. Five large fillets and a couple of bobs' worth should do the trick.

RIGGIE. I love fish and chips.

TONY. (*Crosses to above sofa.*) While you get the food, Vera can lay the table and John and I will prepare the liquid. We'll have a banquet . . .

RIGGIE. (*To* SIMON.) I'll come with you.

SIMON. (*Nervously.*) That's all right—I can manage . . .

TONY. (*Crosses to between* RIGGIE *and* SIMON, *facing* SIMON.) Take her along, old lad. She won't eat you—she's after the chips. (*Pushes* SIMON *on his way,* RIGGIE *follows at his heels.*)

SIMON. (*Crosses to door followed by* RIGGIE.) Okay then . . .

(*When* RIGGIE *has passed him* JOHN *rises, takes a step to her.* RIGGIE *turns to him as he speaks.* JOHN *opens door.*)

JOHN. I say, Riggie, you didn't ought to come back. If Matron gets wind of it . . .

RIGGIE. Pooh! (*Runs round* SIMON *to his* R., *in doorway.*)

TONY. (*Crossing down to* JOHN'S L.) John, don't be so ungallant.

JOHN. (*Turning* L. *to face* TONY.) Look here, Tony, the last bloke who was caught with a nurse in his room copped the lot, you know that.

TONY. Life is a gamble, old chap. Off with you, Simon.

(SIMON *turns to door to find* RIGGIE *right next to him, gazing up at him.*)

RIGGIE. (*To* SIMON.) Do you think one piece of fish each will be enough?

TONY. Dear Riggie . . . always remember the fundamentals. We will leave it to you.

RIGGIE. (*To* SIMON.) Come on then . . . (*She pulls the embarrassed* SIMON *out by the hand.*)

(JOHN *closes the door after them, comes in* L. *a pace.*)

VERA. Tony—what are you up to?

TONY. A mission of goodwill. Vera, clear the decks. (VERA *rises.*) John—rake up all the booze you can find.

JOHN. O.K. (*Goes above sofa to his room* U. L., *opens door, turns on light.*)

VERA. I asked you a question. What are you up to?

TONY. (*Pushes* VERA *up to the top of table.*) My darling, isn't it obvious? We have on our hands one Simon Sparrow.

VERA. I like him.

TONY. We all like him. (*Standing on* VERA'S R. *he picks up Gray's "Anatomy," puts it in her hands, then picking up two other books which are on the table, piles them on top.*) But let's face it. The lad is inhibited. He needs broadening. His outlook is too serious.

VERA. He just wants to be a doctor.

TONY. (*Crosses down to in front of sofa.* JOHN *switches off light and closes bedroom door behind him.*) I don't blame him for that. But we shouldn't allow it to blight his whole life.

JOHN. (*Comes in carrying a pint bottle of beer and a*

bottle of advocaat which he places on the table, R. *of* VERA.) Hang it all, Vera, Tony's right. The fellow ducked a rugger trial this afternoon. To put it at its mildest, that's pretty rotten bad taste. (*Crosses above sofa.*)

VERA. Perhaps he doesn't like rugger.

JOHN. (*Turns back to* VERA *above sofa.*) He's not as abnormal as all that. He was a cracking three-quarter at school. Anyway we need him (*Goes to bookshelves in recess above door* D R.)

VERA. I'm not going to stand by and see you make a fool of him. (*Carries books to piano, puts them on closed keyboard lid.*)

TONY. (*Crosses up to* VERA *to kiss her.*) My darling, my pigeon I want to help the lad. (*Goes* L *of* VERA *taking off jacket, which he puts on window seat of* U. S. *window after drawing back one of the curtains.*) John —get weaving with that booze. (JOHN *takes bottle of crème de menthe and whisky from shelves and goes into bedroom* U. R. *Light on.*)

VERA. (*Turns to face* TONY.) I am warning you, Tony. He is a nice person—if you spoil him . . . (*She then gets five small glasses from top of piano.*)

TONY. Trust me. (*Picks up a large Pyrex bowl and kitchen ladle off window seat. Brings them to above table on* VERA'S L., *puts the bowl on table brandishing the ladle aloft as he quotes.*) It is a far, far better thing I do now than I have ever done. (JOHN *enters, carrying bottles: crème de menthe, whisky, beer and wine. Crosses to table*) It is a far, far better place I . . . What have we got, John?

JOHN. (*Puts all but wine bottle down on table. He is on* TONY'S R.) Half a bottle of brown, one of light, a drain of crème de menthe, advocaat, whisky.

TONY. What's that wine?

JOHN. It's got sediment in it . . .

(TONY *takes wine from* JOHN. VERA *comes down to*

JOHN'S R., *bringing the glasses which she puts on table. She and* TONY *undo the stoppers and corks.*)

TONY. Adds to the flavour, old boy. What else? Gin?
JOHN. No gin.
TONY. We had some gin. Vera, my pigeon, what happened to the gin?
VERA. Why ask me?
TONY. You had it last . . . Wait . . . look under the bed, John. (JOHN *gives a quick look at* TONY *then at* VERA, *shrugs and goes off again* U. R. *With a bottle in each hand* TONY *pours the contents into the bowl, two by two The mixture changing colour, yellow, orange, green*) Secretus, secretorum, tu operus sis secretus horum. I adjure and command you, ye strong and mighty spirits, to obey me in my cause. (*The bowl now full he brandishes the ladle aloft.*) I conjure thee, spirits.

JOHN. (*Puts out bedroom light, closes the door, crosses to below table*) Here we are . . . (*Crosses round below table up the* L *side of it to* TONY'S L , *taking the cap off the gin bottle which he is carrying.*) Hey, what are you making?

TONY. A St. Swithin's special. Known in the Highlands as Grimsdyke Punch. (*Takes the gin from* JOHN, *pours it in.*)

JOHN. Ooh—*ooh!*
TONY. (*Tasting it from the ladle.*) Too much beer. We need some sherry . . . Vera, any sherry?

VERA. Some cheap stuff I bought for cooking.

TONY. Bring it, woman. (VERA *goes down to* R. *side of table, below it to under* D. S. *window seat where she finds a bottle of cooking sherry. Returns up the* L. *side of table behind* JOHN *and across the top behind* TONY *to* TONY'S R. *She takes the top off sherry bottle.*) Of course, what it really needs to give it a kick is a dog's tooth, a sparrow's brain, some pigeon's liver, arsenic, sulphur, rum, and the blood of a black cat (*Grabs sherry from* VERA, *pours it in. Lifting it high above the bowl, laughs diabolically*)

He, he, he, he'' It came from outer space! (*He tastes it, smacking his lips.*) Mmm . . . Now this really has something . . . Try it . . .

(VERA *and* JOHN *each dip in a small glass and try it.*)

JOHN. (*Yells as though in violent pain.*) Owww! (*Spins round and sits on stool, back to table, gasping.*) Crikey . . .
VERA. (*Very calmly*) *I* think you've spoiled the gin.
TONY. I have it' Tomato juice— (JOHN *still on the stool turns* U. S. *to face* TONY, *a look of disgust on his face.*) that might stiffen it a little.
VERA. We haven't any.
TONY. This'll do the trick. (*Turns* U. S., *sees tomato sauce on the piano, goes to get it, brings it to the table, takes off cap, pours it into the mixture, dips the glass in and tastes it. Smacks his lips with pleasure. Puts glass down.*) Mm! mm! mm!
JOHN. (*Dips his glass in the bowl and drinks it.*) I think I'll try some more.
VERA. Me, too . . . (*Helps herself.*)
TONY. Hold up. Don't swig the lot . . .
JOHN. It's not bad . . .
TONY. Wonderful what you can whip together when you try. Happy now?
JOHN. (*In a descending scale.*) Ha, ha, ha, ha, ha, ha'
TONY. (*Turning it into the song.*) He, he, he,
ALL. (*Sing.*)
        Little brown jug don't I love thee,
        Ha, ha, ha, you and me,
        Little brown jug don't I love thee.
TONY. (*Sings, puts his* R. *arm round* VERA'S *shoulder.*) She sighed (*They both take a step to the* R. *to between table and sofa.*) She cried.
VERA. (*Sings, lays her head on* TONY'S *shoulder, acting the line.*) She darn near died,

(JOHN *moves to* TONY'S L. *He and* VERA *still have their glasses.* TONY *puts his* L. *arm round* JOHN'S *shoulder.*)

JOHN. She said, "What shall I do oo-oo?"

ALL. (*Sing.*) So I took (*All take a step down with the* R. *foot.*) her into bed (*Step with the* L. *foot.*) And I (*Step with the* R. *foot.*) covered up her head, (*Step with the* L. *foot.*) Just to save (TONY *puts* R. *foot up on pouffe.*) her from the foggy, (JOHN *puts* R. *foot up on pouffe.*) foggy, dew. (VERA *puts* R. *foot up on pouffe.*)

JOHN. (*Sings this line in harmony while others hold the last note.*) The foggy dew-oo!

(VERA *finishes off with an* "ooh" *an octave higher. Then all laugh.* RIGGIE *enters* R. *to below* R. *of sofa followed by* SIMON *who closes door.* TONY *comes back to table and fills two glasses from the bowl.* SIMON *crosses to sofa table, puts chips on it, returns to in front of door.* RIGGIE *also has a little bag of sweets.*)

RIGGIE. I can smell burning.

JOHN. That's the lining of my stomach! (JOHN *crosses* L. *to below table, turns to face* SIMON, *raising his glass.* RIGGIE *puts her chips down on the table behind sofa.*) Simon, allow me to introduce you to St. Swithin's Special.

RIGGIE. I'm hungry . . .

TONY. Everything in its proper place, (*Crosses to between* SIMON *and* RIGGIE *with two glasses of punch.*) Riggie. Liquid first. (*Hands* RIGGIE *a glass then* SIMON.) Simon—here you are . . .

SIMON. (*Standing* D. R. *below armchair, doesn't take the glass.*) Er . . . I don't think so.

TONY. Aw, come on. We laid this on specially for you. (*Hands* SIMON *the glass which he takes dubiously.*)

VERA. It's quite harmless, Simon. (*Takes a drink, staggers slightly and lands, sitting on the pouffe, facing* SIMON.)

RIGGIE. (*Raises her glass.*) Bottoms up! (*Drinks it down with no effect.*) Doesn't do anything to me.
SIMON. (*Warily.*) What is it?

(JOHN *sits on the* D. S. *edge of the table.*)

TONY. A medicinal mixture, old boy. Made from an old recipe I got from an ancient farmer in the Highlands. Guaranteed to bring the roses to your cheeks. One sip and never a dull moment.
SIMON. What's in it?
TONY. You might fairly describe it as a sort of lemonade cocktail. I give you my solemn assurance that one glass of this will make you feel not merely happy—but ecstatic . . .
JOHN. (*Crossing* R., *behind* VERA *to* RIGGIE'S L.) Come on, feller—in for a penny, in for a pound. (*Raises his glass.*) Cheers . . .
TONY. (*Raises his.*) Cheers!
SIMON. (*Raises his.*) Cheers . . . (*He drains the glass.*)
TONY. Well?
SIMON. Mild enough . . .
TONY. Fill him up again, John.

(TONY *brings* SIMON *to top of table.* SIMON *on his* R. JOHN *follows, goes behind them to* U. L. *corner of table.* VERA *crosses behind table to* L. *side of it, standing below* JOHN. RIGGIE *comes to* D. S. *of table and when she has filled her glass, goes* R. *of table.*)

ALL. (*Ad lib.*) Another little drink won't do you any harm. Give him another, etc., etc. (*The glasses are recharged, and they all drink.*)
TONY. (*Fills* SIMON'S *glass, hands it to him.*) Here you are, Simon, down the hatch!
SIMON. (*Drinks it down.*) I like it.

TONY. He likes it!
JOHN. (*Singing*)
  Caviare comes from virgin sturgeon,
ALL. (*Except* SIMON.)
  A virgin sturgeon's a very fine fish.
  A virgin sturgeon needs no urgin',
  That's why caviare is my dish.
SIMON. (*Taking it up as he steps back a pace to the* R.)
  I gave caviare to my girl friend,
    (*The others stop.*)
  She was a virgin tried and true;
  Now my girl friend needs no urgin',
  There is nothing she won't do.

(SIMON *bends down and says* "Boo!" *loudly into* RIGGIE'S *face. All laugh and applaud* SIMON. RIGGIE *puts her glass down on table.*)

TONY. Bravo. (*Puts arm round* SIMON *and brings him to top of table again, and refills his glass.*) Here . . . (*To* VERA.) Can't you see our Simon opening out?
SIMON. I shouldn't drink on an empty stomach. (*He drinks.*)
TONY. Only way *to* drink, old lad. Too expensive t'other way.
RIGGIE. (*Sits on pouffe facing them.*) I'm hungry.
TONY. One track mind.
SIMON. I'm going to like being a medical student. It's a wonderful life . . .
JOHN. (*Singing. Sings a very long* "Oh" *over the end of* SIMON'S *line,* JOHN *and* VERA *put glasses down.*)
  Oh you push the damper in,
    (*Gesture away from him.* ALL *join in.*)
  And you pull the damper out,
    (*Gesture towards him,* VERA *doing the same. Meanwhile* TONY *explains to* SIMON "This is a dance we all do." *They put their glasses down* VERA *and* JOHN *wagging first finger of* R. *hand in the air come down*

ACT I   DOCTOR IN THE HOUSE   45

*to L. of pouffe. JOHN above, VERA below. RIGGIE
turns on pouffe to face front and eats sweets from
her paper bag. TONY brings SIMON down to R. of
pouffe. SIMON above, TONY below.)*
And the smoke goes up the chimney just the same.
You push the damn thing in,
*(Clapping hands they advance to pouffe, then clap
with person facing. TONY shouts "In.")*
And you pull the damn thing out,
(Clapping hands they retreat, TONY says "Out.")
And the smoke goes up the chimney just the same.
*(TONY sings "All hands now!" They join hands in a
ring and revolve round RIGGIE in a clockwise direction. RIGGIE pays no attention, eats her sweets.
TONY gives SIMON an odd kick as they circle.)*
  Campha . . . campha . . . amphorated,
  Campha . . . ampha . . amphorated,
  Campha . . . ampha . . amphorated,
And we washed him out with camphorated oil.

*(TONY and JOHN lift VERA in the air in front of sofa.
Tum, tiddely-om-pom, pom-pom. Drop her on sofa.
Meanwhile SIMON has run up behind sofa to U. R. C.
RIGGIE blows her paper bag and "pops" it.)*

RIGGIE. When are we going to eat?
TONY. Just one for the road . . .

*(TONY runs to top of table, refills his own glass and then
crosses R. to SIMON. JOHN goes to L. of table, refills
his glass, crosses to sofa, climbs on to U. S. end of
it, putting his glass on table behind it.)*

SIMON. *(Claps hands loudly, then sings.)*
  She was poor but she was honest,
  Victim of a rich man's whim,
  First he loved her, then he left her,
  And she bore a child by him.

(JOHN *does a "fill-in" like a trumpet.* TONY *gives* SIMON *a glass.* SIMON *drinks.*)

It's the same the whole world over,
It's the poor what gets the blame,
It's the rich what gets the gravy,
Ain't it all a blinking shame.
(*Trumpet again.*)

(SIMON *recites.*)

In the street of a thousand lanterns . . .
Where the reek of the . . .
(*Breaks off, clutches stomach, crosses down to in front of armchair.*)

TONY. (*Puts glass on sofa table then a pace down to* L. *of armchair.*) Carry on, old boy. What's wrong? (RIGGIE *rises, gets chips from sofa table.*)

SIMON. In the street of a thousand lanterns . . .

(RIGGIE, *disgusted by the delay, brings over a packet of fish for* SIMON. *She holds it, unwrapped, under his nose.*)

RIGGIE. Cod or rock-salmon?

(SIMON *reels a little, flops down in the chair, helped by* TONY, *waving the fish aside. With a shrug* RIGGIE *starts to eat it herself, sitting on* R. *arm of sofa.*)

VERA. Are you all right, Simon?
SIMON. I feel awfully pecu . . . peculiar.
JOHN. It must be something you drank.
SIMON. Everything seems so unsteady . . . Odd . . . What happened to me?

(TONY *puts his glass down on sofa table, lifts* SIMON *up, bringing him down below armchair.* SIMON *on the* R., TONY *on the* L. *facing each other.*)

TONY. (*Cheerfully.*) Simply a case of released inhibition, old lad. You'll be all right now. A glorious future stretches before you . . .

(RIGGIE *starts to sing* "Caviare" *joined by* VERA. JOHN *"plays" accompaniment as a "bag-pipe" solo.*)

SIMON. But what happened?
TONY. You've been blooded, old boy, blooded.

(TONY *and* SIMON *put their arms round each other and and joining in the chorus of* "Caviare comes from a virgin sturgeon" *they dance across the front of the stage.*)

CURTAIN

PROLOGUE TO ACT TWO

TONY *appears before the curtain, holding a glass of beer in one hand.*

TONY. Cheers! Well, we managed to scrape through our anatomy exams by the skin of our teeth and they let us loose in the hospital proper. Believe me, it takes a strong stomach to stand it. We were classified as clerks . . . which is just about the lowest category of human life existing on God's earth. As far as the senior doctors were concerned we were just a bloody nuisance, and the Matron—she looked upon us as a bunch of maniacs who were out to chase every nurse in the place. Still, we managed to survive, which is more than one can say for some of the patients. Old Simon was really beginning to enjoy himself. He was blooded, all right. Except . . . well, except that in one direction his youthful innocence still dogged his footsteps. It was a great problem to me. And it led us into one or two rather difficult situations . . . However, you shall see. Here we are, then, a couple of years later . . . at Christmas . . . don't go away . . . (*He goes behind the tabs, which rise a moment later on Act Two.*)

ACT TWO

The same. Evening, a day or so before Christmas.

The curtains are closed, the lamps and light are on. "Charley" the skeleton has been hung on a hook R. of the drinks cabinet. There is a small Christmas tree with decorations on it on the corner cupboard U L. The stool is at the R of the table, chair at the L. Chair from D. L is in front of the corner cupboard U. L. Holly behind the pictures.

It is snowing outside. From the direction of the room U. R. *we can hear* VERA *singing a carol "Noel."* SIMON, *looking far more disreputable than before, i.e much more like a medical student, is seated above the table, looking in the microscope. As we shall see, his manner is in keeping with his appearance. He has been blooded.* JOHN EVANS *enters, banging the snow from his boots. He hangs his duffle coat on the back of the door, walks over to the sofa and sits* C. *of it with a sigh.*

SIMON. What-ho, stinker.
JOHN. Hi.
SIMON. How goes it?
JOHN. I'm done in. Why do women have to have babies? Why can't they just bud, like flowers?
SIMON. You've been called out? But that's wonderful.
JOHN. Glad you think so. You wait until you take your midwifery course. It's no picnic, let me tell you.
SIMON. You've only been on it for twenty-four hours.

(VERA *enters from* U. R. *carrying a cardboard box with tinsel in it crossing to* L. *above sofa.*)

JOHN. Twenty-four hours too long.
SIMON. Vera, (VERA *stops between sofa and table.*) what do you think? Our John is a father—almost.
VERA. (*Excitedly*) You don't mean . . . oh, John, you've had your first confinement. That's wonderful . . . Tell me what it was like . . .
JOHN. What for?
VERA. What for? I shall be a mother one day, of course.
SIMON. You're not . . . I mean, Vera, you aren't . . .
VERA. Of course not, silly. I mean I intend to become a mother. At some future date. And naturally I want to know all about it.

JOHN. I think you've got all the necessary qualifications, dear.

VERA Be sensible. (*She crosses to* JOHN, *sits on* U. S. *arm of sofa.*) John—don't you realize? You've helped to bring a young life into the world. You've really been a doctor—a proper doctor—for a few hours. Doesn't that make you feel good?

JOHN. No.

VERA. (*Rises.*) Oh, don't be so cynical. I bet you felt as proud as a . . . as a . . .

SIMON *and* JOHN. (*Together.*) Peacock.

(VERA *smiles a* "thank you" *to them for the word.*)

JOHN. (*Seriously.*) As a matter of fact, I felt a bit of a worm. As though I was there under false pretences.

VERA. I bet you were marvellous, calm, and cool, and efficient. (*She crosses* U. L. *to the Xmas tree and climbs on the chair.*)

JOHN. I wasn't, you know. I was in a cold sweat.

SIMON. It wasn't a B.B.A.?

VERA. (*On the chair putting tinsel on the tree.*) What's a B.B.A.?

JOHN. Born before arrival. No—but it was a jolly near thing. First thing that happened was that the bloody bicycle broke down. I left it in the snow like a dead husky and walked two miles.

VERA. I saw a film in which the doctor did that.

JOHN. I kept thinking—it'll be all right, the midwife will be there to do the real work. Just my luck! She was snowbound and didn't show up!

VERA. (*Leaving the box on the corner cupboard she climbs down and comes to corner of table on* SIMON'S R.) So you did it single-handed. All the more credit to you, John.

JOHN. Hmph. It was lucky the mother was there.

SIMON. Isn't there always a mother present in such cases?

ACT II DOCTOR IN THE HOUSE 51

(VERA *gives* SIMON *a push, he ducks away, laughing. She then comes back to* U. S. *arm of sofa, leans on it.*)

JOHN. Shut up. This one was a brick. She took one look at me as I went into the bedroom and said: "Don't worry, young man. I've had five others, so I know something about it." And so, with her help, and a little shoving from Le Bon Dieu, we carried it off.

VERA You must be tired out, you poor thing. (*Comes down to* JOHN'S *level, swivels his feet up on to the* D. S. *end of sofa, goes round the sofa and off into room* U. R. JOHN *rests his head on* U. S. *sofa arm.*) You sit there and put your feet up and I'll get you a nice cup of tea. Tu vois comme je suis une brave fille, hein?

JOHN. Mais oui, oui, oui. (SIMON, *with a sigh, puts his feet up on stool*) What's up with you?

SIMON. Nothing. I just feel sort of lethargic.

JOHN You mean browned-off?

SIMON. Sort of. Hey-ho—what is life . . .

JOHN. Simon, I noticed you were off your game last Saturday. You sickening for something?

SIMON. Not that I know of. The fact is—I don't sleep properly. Dreams and all that.

JOHN. (*Putting on a "learned voice" and leaning up on* L. *arm to face* SIMON.) There are, of course, two kinds of sleep. Shallow sleep and deep sleep. What you need is a nice hot cup of . . .

SIMON. Shut up, you clot. I was wondering, actually, if my libido was subnormal . . .

JOHN. (*Horrified.*) Your what?

SIMON. My libido. Or perhaps I'm suffering from oral eroticism . . .

JOHN. Or simply chicken pox. What are you jabbering about, you ass?

(TONY *kicks the door open and comes in briskly. He wears an old frock coat over his shoulders, and an old-fashioned black topper at a rakish angle.*)

TONY. Greetings, most reverend seigneurs. (*He bows gracefully as he comes to behind sofa, "acting" madly* SIMON *puts his feet down again.*) Aha, aha. But an hour since I saw your father—a pitiful relic of the proud man he once was—grovelling in the snow. And what brought him there, my proud beauty? Drink! (VERA *enters from* U. R., *comes down behind* TONY *to between armchair and sofa.*) Yes, the devil's brew has brought him low! (TONY *throws coat on to divan.*)

VERA. Tony!

TONY. (*Turns to face* VERA.) What have we here? Ah, your daughter. (*Aside.*) She shall not escape the malignant coruscations of my illimitable seductions. (*To* VERA, *pulling her by her* L. *arm behind sofa.*) In short, and to be brief, I have you in my power. (VERA *knocks off his topper.*) Steady, old girl. (*He picks up the hat.*) That's a valuable stage prop. It has to be returned in good condition.

VERA. Do you want any tea?

TONY. The cup that cheers? What a thoughtful little woman it is. (*Kisses* VERA.)

VERA. Kettle's just boiling. (*Exit* U. R.)

TONY (*Crossing above sofa to* SIMON.) And now, gentlemen, if I may have your undivided attention. I have a scheme to unfold. . . .

JOHN. Pipe down a minute, Tony. Old Simon was just in the middle of telling me his sad story.

TONY. A confession? (*To sofa table, puts his hat on it.*)

JOHN. Uh-huh.

SIMON. I just happened to pick up a book on psychology, and one or two things in it seemed to fit my case.

TONY. Crikey. (*Leans over back of sofa* U. S. *end* JOHN *puts feet down and moves up sofa to* U. S. *end.*)

SIMON. You won't laugh if I tell you?

TONY. Cross my heart. See, that's wet, see, that's dry . . .

SIMON. All right. Only I am serious—in a way. (*He

ACT II   DOCTOR IN THE HOUSE   53

pauses, rises and crosses R. *to* U. S. *corner of sofa.*) You see (TONY *and* JOHN *gaze at him in deadly earnest. He looks at them, looks away disconcerted, makes an effort and starts again.*) Well—I'm beginning to think there's something funny about me.

JOHN. Truth will out.

SIMON. (*Furiously.*) If you're going to make rotten jokes . . .

JOHN. Sorry. It slipped out.

TONY. (*To* SIMON.) Press on, old boy. Let's have the symptoms.

SIMON. Well, it's like this . . . (*The door opens and* BROMLEY *comes in*) Oh, hell . . .

BROMLEY. (*At door to* TONY.) I've got 'em, sir . . .

TONY. (*Crossing to below armchair.*) Come in, my old Bromley.

(BROMLEY *enters. He carries a case and six small scripts.*
    BROMLEY *goes to behind armchair* D. R., *puts case and scripts down.*)

SIMON. (*Bitterly, crossing to* TONY'S L.) Come in, Bromley. Got any friends? Bring 'em in, too . . . Bring all the medical students and the staff . . .

BROMLEY. (*Coming down* R. *side of armchair to* TONY'S R., *putting on his hat.*) Naturally, sir, if I find myself unwelcome . . .

TONY. (*Takes* BROMLEY'S *hat off and puts it in his hand.*) What nonsense. Step nearer, Bromley. I shall need you later. And in the meantime you can bring your vast experience of life to bear on Mr. Sparrow's problems.

(BROMLEY *goes behind armchair again, takes off his coat and drops hat and coat on top of his case, returns to* TONY'S R.)

SIMON. If you think I'm going . . .

TONY. (*Turning to* SIMON.) Bromley will be invaluable. (JOHN *moves down sofa to* D. S *end of it watching the others over the arm.*) I think I know what's wrong with you, old boy. And Bromley will be able to confirm my opinion. (TONY *passes* BROMLEY *across him to* SIMON'S R.)

BROMLEY. A sort of professional consultant. (*Looking closely at* SIMON.) And something *is* wrong with you, sir. Make no bones about that. Couldn't be clearer if it was written in blood on your face.

SIMON. I *look* bad?

BROMLEY. Well—not bad exactly, sir. A certain strain shows in the eyes. (*Steps up* L. *side of armchair*)

TONY So here we are. At your service, Simon. (*Steps to* R. *side of armchair, gestures to chair.*) Continue!

SIMON. (*Sits in armchair*) We-ell . . . Okay. What I want to know is this—what *is* there about me that makes women duck for cover when they see me coming?

BROMLEY. If I might interject, Mr Sparrow . . .

JOHN. You might not . . .

(BROMLEY *shrugs, goes* U. S, *picks his coat and hat up on the way and lays them on the divan.*)

SIMON. In the last few months I've tried to date about six different women—nurses mostly . . .

TONY. Ah, I thought so

SIMON. You thought what?

TONY. (*To top of armchair.*) Never mind. (*Down the* L. *side of it to between* JOHN *and* SIMON.) Forward, my boy.

(BROMLEY *comes down to* R. *of armchair.*)

SIMON. In every case, something has gone haywire. First one was that little snub-nosed brunette probationer.

JOHN Lovely little thing.

BROMLEY. I remember her well. As I understand it, when you spoke to her she had only been in the hospital two or three weeks.

SIMON. That's right.

TONY. What the dickens did you say?

SIMON It was in the sluice-room. She came in to clean out the sink . . .

JOHN. A romantic beginning . . .

SIMON. I approached her. She smiled. I didn't know quite what to say . . .

TONY. But you said something?

SIMON. Of course I did. I made some innocuous remark about an operation.

TONY. An innocuous remark about an operation? What did you want to do—remove the girl's gall bladder?

BROMLEY. (*Arms on* R. *arm of chair leaning over* SIMON.) Can you remember what you said, sir? It's helpful in such cases . . . (*Straightens up again.*)

SIMON. Oh . . . I think I remarked that one of the patients was looking better . . . No, I know . . . I told her what a good job the Chief had done in surgery. It was pretty impressive. You should have seen the way he got hold of the splenic artery when a clip came off. I've never seen so much blood in all my life.

(*There is a little silence while the others look at each other, then at* SIMON.)

TONY. That . . . er . . . was your opening gambit?

SIMON. More or less.

JOHN. Did she respond?

SIMON. She fainted.

TONY. (*Puts his hand to his forehead, closing his eyes in mock horror.*) Any more romantic episodes?

SIMON. Well, there was that other nurse—Peggy something-or-other . . . She said she *would* meet me. But she didn't show up. I haven't seen her since.

BROMLEY. I can explain that, sir. She was rather overcome by circumstances one day and threw a pink blancmange at Sister Virtue.

TONY. I heard it was a brown blancmange. Chocolate, in fact.

BROMLEY. (*A pace* U. S. *to speak to* TONY.) I can assure you it was pink, sir. And it hadn't properly set. (*Back to his original position.*)

TONY. Hm . . . I suppose the actual colour is immaterial. Have you completed your testimony, Simon?

SIMON. More or less. I've had other dates, but they've never shown any eagerness to repeat the experience. Have I got a mother-fixation? Or oral-eroticism—is my testosterone subnormal?

TONY. Come here! (*Takes a pace* L., *beckons to* SIMON *who rises, stands in front of him facing him* L., *turns to look at* BROMLEY. TONY *straightens him again.*) Stand still . . . Tongue out, (SIMON *puts tongue out a little way.*) please—right out.

(SIMON *puts it right out.* TONY *looks at it horrified, comes to below armchair beckoning to* BROMLEY *who crosses above him, below chair.* TONY *stands below* R. *of chair watching.* BROMLEY *goes to* SIMON, *looks at* SIMON *in horror, clicks his fingers, in front of* SIMON'S *tongue*, SIMON *puts it in again. Placing two fingers on* R. *side of* SIMON'S *chest, puts his ear to them. Repeats operation on other side of chest. Placing hands on* SIMON'S *arms he leans close, his* R *ear against* SIMON'S *heart. Looks up at him dismayed. Signals despair to* TONY, *crosses to* TONY'S L. *They both clasp hands behind their backs and walk* U. S. R. *of armchair, muttering. By the divan they turn inwards, look at* SIMON, *and resume their tête-à-tête.*)

SIMON. (*Sits on* L. *arm of chair.*) If you're pulling my leg.

(TONY *comes down to* L *of chair, facing* SIMON. BROMLEY *down* R. *side of chair.*)

TONY. (*Seriously.*) My dear old chap, we wouldn't

dream of it. In our considered view you are suffering from that well-known clinical condition orchitis amorosa acuta, lover's nuts.

JOHN. In other words, you need the love and companionship which only a woman can provide.

SIMON. (*Rises.*) I know that, you clot. (*A step* D. S.) What do you think I've been trying to get for the last six months? (*Turns to face* TONY. *At that moment* VERA *enters.*) I'd willingly surrender my honour if I could find someone to co-operate with me in the matter.

(VERA *enters from the room* U. R. *carrying a tray on which are a teapot, milk-jug, four mugs, a bowl of sugar and a teaspoon.*)

VERA. (*Above sofa.*) Can I help?

TONY. (*Crosses to* VERA.) You keep out of this, my pigeon. Your job is to keep down my frustrations, not help him with his.

VERA. (*Crossing to top of table, puts the tray down, pours out the tea.*) I've heard every word you've been saying, and I think you should stop teasing poor Simon.

JOHN. (*Moves along to* C. *of sofa.*) You know, women are the devil, always getting in the way and mucking things up.

TONY. (*Moving down behind the sofa, sits* D. S. *arm.*) All the same, I think women are here to stay. We have to adjust ourselves to that fact.

JOHN. Yes, but you make one move, one tiny little move, and they start dreaming of orange-blossoms and wedding-bells. Vixens, the lot of them. (*Still sitting, does an elaborate bow to* VERA.) Present company excepted.

VERA. Thank you. (*Returns the bow.*) Come and get it.

(BROMLEY *crosses to* R. *of table, sits on stool facing* D. R. SIMON *follows him across, stands* U. R. *of him.* VERA *gives* BROMLEY *a mug of tea.*)

BROMLEY. I'm afraid most of the nurses do have

marriage in view, Mr. Sparrow. I don't think they'd admit it, but that's the main reason they enter our profession.

SIMON. I thought nursing was supposed to be a vocation, a sacred calling.

(VERA *hands two mugs of tea to* SIMON *who passes them across to* JOHN *and* TONY.)

BROMLEY. What you read on the label, sir, ain't always found in the bottle.

SIMON. But what am I to do? I don't want to get married, that's for sure, but I would like to prove to myself that I'm not entirely a monster in their eyes. (*Crosses to sofa, sits* U. S. *arm.*)

(VERA *gives* SIMON *a mug, with the spoon.*)

BROMLEY. Playing with fire, sir.

TONY. What do you suggest, Vera, my pigeon? (*Sits in sofa* D. S. *end.*)

VERA. (*Crossing* R. *to behind* TONY.) I'm not getting involved. In my view, you're a crowd of morons, and if you worked harder and concentrated on your exams, you'd have less time to fill your mind with evil thoughts. (*She pats the top of* TONY's *head and goes off* U. R.)

TONY. (*Calling after her.*) Only to be expected. You're a woman . . . I think!

JOHN. (*To* SIMON.) There *is* a nurse in out-patients—auburn hair, cheeky manner . . .

BROMLEY. (*Rising and crossing to* SIMON *for teaspoon.*) Is she a probationer, sir?

JOHN. Yes, I think so.

BROMLEY. (*Returning to his stool, sits, stirs tea and puts spoon on tray.*) I would advise Mr. Sparrow to avoid the probationers, sir. They're rather young and unappreciative.

TONY. Bromley's right. They're still young enough to remember the games mistress telling them that sex would ruin their hockey. (*A pause.*) How about that little brunette staff nurse on Loftus ward? There's a lovely bit of crackling!

BROMLEY. I have heard, sir, that *she* suffers from tinnitus.

SIMON. (*Rising, crosses to table and puts mug down on tray, back to beside* U. S. *sofa arm.*) Is that bad?

BROMLEY. It's a sort of ringing in the ears, sir.

JOHN. The ringing of wedding bells, old boy.

TONY. Check! (*Rises and crosses to* SIMON'S L., *between sofa and table, faces* SIMON.) I have just the answer. How about old Rigor Mortis?

JOHN. Riggie! Wonderful idea!

TONY. Not a great beauty, Simon, I grant you! But she is not unblessed with attractions, and she has the kindest heart in the world. She expects the minimum of entertainment, has no desire for marriage, and will console you by all the means in her power at the drop of a hat.

JOHN. All you have to do is hold her hand and look plaintive.

BROMLEY. A capital suggestion, sir. The young lady is quite exceptional in many ways.

TONY. How do you know, Bromley? (*Crossing to top of table, puts his mug down.*)

BROMLEY. There is very little that escapes me, sir.

SIMON. Well . . .

TONY. (*Comes to* L. *of* SIMON *again.*) No wells, old boy. Riggie is your medicine. Take her like a man.

JOHN. Three times daily after meals.

BROMLEY. If I might suggest it, sir, a little moderation to begin with.

JOHN. No, the boy's in a bad way, he must grasp the nettle, Bromley. (*Balancing his mug on sofa arm, he kneels up on one knee to speak to* SIMON.) Look here, Simon, meet her one evening about six, whip her into the flicks, back here for a drink—that'll be about-er-nine-thirty. Gives you two solid hours to do your stuff.

TONY. Not necessary, old boy. Riggie's coming here this evening.

SIMON. I don't think I could manage . . .

TONY. (*Crossing to* D. S. *end of sofa.*) You stay here. It's absolutely made to order. We'll all clear off and leave you to it . . . there's a half bottle of gin in the cupboard. That'll start you off.

JOHN. (*Sits* U. S. *end of sofa again.*) What's Riggie coming here for, anyway?

TONY. (*Sits* D. S. *end of sofa.*) For a rehearsal, old boy.

JOHN. Does she *need* a rehearsal? (*Rises, crosses to top of table, cup down, return to* C.)

TONY. Not that, you chump. A rehearsal of our Christmas play.

SIMON. Our what?

TONY. Not what, clot. Say pardon, like a good boy. Bromley, distribute the manuscripts.

BROMLEY. Certainly, sir. (*Rises, crosses below sofa up to behind armchair, picks up the scripts, puts two on* D. S. *sofa arm for* TONY *and* VERA, *gives one to* JOHN, *one for* SIMON, *comes below table to* D. L. *corner, puts* RIGGIE'S *there, stays where he is.* SIMON *sits stool* R. *of table.*)

TONY. You know, every Christmas we put on a show for the patients. Every blooming Christmas it's the same blooming thing. A revue. This year *we* are going to do something different.

JOHN. (*Taking book.*) This? (*Moves down to pouffe as he reads.*) "Don't go out tonight, dear Father"—or "Millicent's Dilemma." (*Sits pouffe, facing* D. S.)

SIMON Good Lord . . .

(BROMLEY *takes a tangled grey wig out of his pocket.*)

TONY. A moral melodrama, my friends. In which the evils of strong drink are exposed to one and all.

SIMON. Couldn't we do Sweeney Todd?

TONY. Most unsuitable. Our surgeons would think we were getting at them. No—this is just the job. We'll paralyse them.

JOHN. (*Reading*) Mother, darling, as you look down from your seat among the angels, pity and forgive your poor, poor daughter Tony, you're not serious.

TONY Perfectly. We shall perform an extract from this epic.

JOHN. It says here—"written by A. Gentleman."

TONY (*Rises.*) Need I say more? Written and performed by gentlemen. Turn to the anthem at the end . . . Now, on the fourth beat . . . (*Conducts them in the song, which he and* BROMLEY *start off, others joining in after a few words. During the song,* BROMLEY, *singing lustily the while, crosses above table round back of sofa, finishing up* R. *of the* D S. *sofa arm*)

>Yield not to temptation,
>For yielding is sin,
>>(TONY.) Louder.
>Try drinking some water
>It's much better than gin.
>>(TONY.) Very softly.
>Strong drink is a demon
>Seeking men to subdue
>>(TONY.) Big, now.
>Water, wonderful water
>Is much better for you.

(TONY *climbs on the sofa, dons the topper, orates as though addressing an audience* BROMLEY *to* L. *of armchair,* JOHN *turns on pouffe to face* TONY.) And, my friends, if there is anyone here who is not a total abstainer you will find stewards in the house with beakers of water. (VERA *enters from* U. R. BROMLEY *puts a finger to his lips,* VERA *tip-toes down to below* R. *of* TONY) We pray you tonight to taste, at our expense, free, gratis and for nothing, the benefit of pure water—Adam's ale, the finest gift of God to suffering humanity . . .

VERA. Is he all right?

TONY. (*Turning to her.*) Do not harden your heart, madam. Let my words awaken an answering chord in your . . chest Abandon liquor ere it be too late, I beg you.

SIMON. Ignore him, Vera. He's nuts. Tony, we can't do it. (*Throws script on table.*)

TONY We can—and we will. I've got it all worked out. Bromley here is going to play Hardy, (BROMLEY *smiles*) the man who is almost ruined by drink (*Looks crestfallen.*) Riggie is going to play Millicent, the daughter. John, my boy, (*Stepping off sofa* TONY *comes down to* JOHN *pointing out character in script*) you'll be handsome Harry, the hero—known as Austin Danesbury.

JOHN. (*Rises, crosses* L *below table, turns to face* TONY) So long as I don't have to put on a dress and stuff rugger socks down my shirt like I did last year I don't mind.

TONY. That privilege is reserved for Simon.

SIMON (*Jumping up.*) Eh?

TONY You have been allotted the role of Mrs. Hardy, the dying wife of the drunkard Bromley—try the costume for size.

BROMLEY. (*Goes behind armchair, undoes case and gets out nightdress.*) Yes, sir!

SIMON No!

TONY Simon—don't spoil everything.

SIMON. (*Backing* L.) I won't do it.

JOHN You'll look gorgeous, Simon, dear. (*He and* TONY *grab* SIMON *and push him* R.)

SIMON. If you think I'm . . . (SIMON D. L. *of armchair,* TONY *on his* L JOHN *next to* TONY)

TONY. There's method in my madness, old boy. As Riggie's mother you will have endless opportunities to embrace your daughter

BROMLEY. There is one scene on your deathbed, sir, which you could really turn to your advantage. (*Bringing nightdress down to* SIMON'S R. *stands in front of him, slipping it over his head. Others crowd in hiding* SIMON *from audience.*)

TONY An absolute sitter, old boy (TONY *takes night-*

cap out of BROMLEY'S R. *pocket, puts it on* SIMON'S *head.*)

SIMON. What about Vera?

VERA. I'm not in the college. No—

BROMLEY. (*Pulling the skirt down.*) We're just trying the costume for size, sir.

(SIMON *wriggles into the nightie which covers him from neck to ankles.* ALL *survey him critically, standing back to reveal him.*)

TONY. He looks like a dish of scrambled eggs around the chest, Bromley.

BROMLEY. (*Grabs the cushion off the armchair, bends down and lifting front of nightdress pushes the cushion up* SIMON *protests loudly.*) This cushion will do the trick, I fancy, sir.

(SIMON, *clasping his middle to keep the cushion up, turns to face* TONY *revealing profile to audience.*)

TONY. He has a big future in front of him.

SIMON. And what about you? I suppose you've kept the best part for yourself?

TONY. (*Sadly.*) How like a woman. I shall produce and direct the show and play Samuel Hepplewhite, the black-hearted villain. (*Acting, aside to* JOHN.) Oh, how I enjoy seeing them writhe. But I have not finished yet. Soon this haughty beauty will be mine, and my revenge will be complete—ha—ha—ha.

SIMON. (*Into* TONY's *face*) Ha—ha—ha!

JOHN. Give him a big kiss, SIMON. *Dear.*

(SIMON *rushes at* JOHN, *who jumps up onto him, hands on his shoulders, legs round his waist. He circles across to below* R. *of sofa,* JOHN *falls off and staggers up back of sofa.*)

TONY. Nark it, nark it.

VERA. (*Still behind table. She puts mugs on the tray.* TONY *is below* R. *of sofa.*) Mind your nightie, Simon.

SIMON. Blast the nightie. (*Crosses below armchair to door.* BROMLEY *goes* U. S. *above armchair, picks up case and puts it on divan.*) I shan't wear the damned thing . . . (*He pulls up the skirt and is about to yank it over his head when* RIGGIE *enters. She stops, somewhat surprised.*)

RIGGIE. Oo, sorry. Didn't know you were dressing.

(RIGGIE *starts to go.* SIMON *goes up* R. *of armchair then down the* R. *side of it again to* TONY.)

TONY. Don't go, Riggie. We were just beginning the rehearsal. Simon—pull your skirt down and behave. You're a grown woman now.

(JOHN *comes down behind* SIMON *and gives his nightdress skirt a tug.* SIMON *lashes out.*)

SIMON. Now look . . .
TONY. All right, all right. No more cracks. Vera, my pigeon, you can be stage-manager. Clear the sofa for a start. Get rid of this table, boys. Now—page twenty-seven, my friends. (TONY *throws script from sofa arm to* VERA. VERA *crosses to drinks cabinet, gets out a tin tray and a large cooking spoon and collects* TONY'S *hat from sofa table.* TONY *turns armchair to face* L. VERA *props tray and spoon against* U. S. *arm on floor, then sits on* U. S. *arm.* TONY *stands* R. *of armchair directing operation.* JOHN *puts the sofa table across the* L. *corner of drinks cabinet then to* U. S. *corner of sofa, pulls it down helping* BROMLEY, *goes to in front of table, kicking pouffe under it.* BROMLEY *puts rug from in front of sofa, straight* U. *and* D. S. R. *of table, goes back to* D. S. *corner of sofa pushing the sofa with* JOHN'S *help* D S *and square on to audience. Goes back to table for two scripts, gives one to* SIMON, *the other to* RIGGIE. *Both are now on sofa. Goes*

behind sofa to VERA, *discusses script with her.* RIGGIE *takes off coat, hat and scarf, leaves them with her bag on small chair below door* D. R. *then to* L. *end of sofa as directed by* TONY. TONY *puts* SIMON *in sofa sitting up at* R. *end, his feet up on* L. *end. He sits* RIGGIE *on* L. *end. Stands at* R. *end himself.*) You—Simon—are lying in bed, ill. Your husband is out on the booze as usual. Your beautiful daughter, Millicent, sits by your bedside—that's you, Riggie. Right—fire away, old boy—and give it bags of expression.

SIMON. (*Pushes up the cushion which has slipped down.*) My bosom keeps slipping.

(JOHN *goes up* R. *side of table, takes off jacket, putting it round back of chair above table, then goes to corner cupboard* U. L., *gets a straw boater hat out of it, returns to* D. L. *corner of table, and sits on it, putting hat on table.*)

TONY. We'll tie it on with string when we do it properly. O.K. get on with it. (*Sits in armchair* D. R.)

SIMON. I think I almost hear the sound of the angel voices, Millicent, they are calling me, calling me.

BROMLEY. (*Coming to between* TONY *and* SIMON, *sings.*) Jerusalem, Jerusalem, lift up your voice and . . .

TONY. BROMLEY!

BROMLEY. Yes, sir?

TONY. What's that for?

BROMLEY. It's the angel voices, sir. Thought it was rather in my line.

TONY. Later. Push on, Millicent.

(BROMLEY *retires* U. S.)

RIGGIE. Who—me?

TONY. Yes, you, you clot. Give her the cue, Simon.

SIMON. They are calling me, calling me . . .

RIGGIE. (*Very flat, no expression.*) I hear nothing, Mother—oh, Mother—cling to me, cling to me . . .

(Simon *grabs her violently, pulling her right along sofa to him. She accepts placidly.*)

Tony. (*Yelling.*) Not like that, you idiot. You're on your deathbed not your blasted honeymoon.

Simon. But you said . . .

Tony. (*Rises, a step to* Simon.) All in good time, old chap This is a rehearsal. Now—try and die like a good woman. (*Sits again.*)

Simon. I am so cold, so cold.

Riggie. Hush, Mother, hush . . . we have no more blankets . . .

Simon Now I am hot, so hot. (*To* Tony.) You know, this damn woman can't make up her mind.

Tony. (*Rises, step to* Simon.) It's the wanderings of a dying woman, you big oaf. And Riggie—try and put some expression into it. Like this. (*Kneeling in front of sofa, speaks into* Simon's *face.* Simon *puts head back*) Hush, Mother, hush. (*Rises, crosses to behind* r. *end of sofa.*)

Riggie. (*Kneels in front of* Simon *for line then sits sofa again.*) Hush, Mother, hush.

Tony. Let it pass. Stand by, John. You enter here . . . (*Returns to armchair, sits again*)

(Vera *rises, picks up tray and spoon.* John *gets off table, puts his hat on.* Vera *bangs on the tray with the spoon, three times, very hard, then sits again.*)

Simon. Hark—do I hear a knocking?

Riggie. (*Very flat, no expression*) I will go and see who is without, Mother, dear. (*She rises, trots* l. *to in front of* John *just as he is going to "make his entrance" as he advances to* l. *corner of sofa She backs, still facing him, hits against sofa and sits.*)

John. It is I, Mr. Austin Danesbury, who thus intrudes in your hour of anguish . . .

Riggie. (*The whole speech in one breath, absolutely*

flat and expressionless.) Oh how good it is to see the face of a dear friend at this moment, Mr. Austin—I fear my mother is past all saving—she calls for Father—and he will not come . .

TONY. (*Rises, crosses to R. corner of sofa*) Riggie— you've got to give it all you've got. (*He hams it madly.*) She calls for Father—and he will not come. See?

RIGGIE. (*The same voice.*) She calls for Father and he will not come I fear I am on the horns of a dilemma. Is that better?

TONY. Not noticeably. But press on. (*Returns to chair, sits*)

SIMON. (*Pointing to* JOHN.) Millicent, who is that?

RIGGIE. It is Mr. Austin Danesbury, Mother.

SIMON Mr. Austin—Millicent—quickly—my bawl.

VERA. What does she want a ball for?

(ALL *look at scripts, puzzled.*)

TONY. (*Rises, crosses to* SIMON, *points to the word in his own script.*) It's not bawl, Simon—*shawl*.

SIMON. Quickly, my shawl.

(JOHN *crosses to statue* R. *of sofa which has a towel round it. Comes down to behind sofa, hands* SIMON *the towel during the speech.* SIMON *puts it round his shoulders angrily.*)

JOHN Know this, Mrs. Hardy, that I regard your daughter as the purest, most tender, most undefiled creature on this earth, and that it is my most humble and ardent wish that she should be . . .

RIGGIE. Oh, Mr Austin—heed what you are saying.

JOHN Nay, I shall not heed.

SIMON. Headstrong boy. (*Giving* JOHN *a dig in the stomach* JOHN *frowns at him, crosses round* R. *end of sofa, kneels at corner to* RIGGIE.)

TONY. Simon!

SIMON. What?
TONY. Serious.
JOHN. Millicent, will you be my bride?
RIGGIE (*In a flatter voice than ever*) Oh ecstasy, oh, joy, joy, joy, joy.
TONY. (*Rises, steps in to sofa.*) Crikey, Riggie—you're supposed to be happy.
RIGGIE (*Rises.*) I can't help it. I think it's soppy.
TONY. It's supposed to be soppy.
RIGGIE. Pooh! (*Crosses in front of* JOHN *tripping over rug to below table.*)
TONY Press on, John. (*Returns to chair, sits.*)
JOHN. (*Rises, steps* R *to* SIMON) Millicent—your poor mother—she has gone cold. (*Hand on* SIMON's *head, steps* D. R. *of him.*)
RIGGIE. Hold her, Austin, hold her.

(JOHN *goes behind* SIMON's *head to embrace him.*)

SIMON. (*Dodging* JOHN's *heavy embrace and pushing him* D S.) Oh, no you don't.
TONY. Come on, Simon. (TONY *rises, crosses to* SIMON, *puts him back in position.* JOHN *returns to* R. *of sofa.* TONY *sits again.*)
SIMON. Millicent—I die—I die. Oh, Millicent—be good, that you might earn the right to come to me.

(SIMON *dies realistically.* BROMLEY *to behind* R *end of sofa. Hums "Hearts and Flowers" loudly.* RIGGIE *runs to sofa. Kneels on it, her bottom in the air, facing audience, and clasping* SIMON. *She then sits again.*)

JOHN. In the midst of life we are in death, Millicent.
VERA. Mr. Hardy—Bromley, you're on.

(BROMLEY, *apologizing, runs across to below table, puts on his wig, and lurches drunkenly up to behind sofa. He really gives it everything.*)

ACT II   DOCTOR IN THE HOUSE   69

BROMLEY. Too late, too late—she has gone—she has gone—while I was drinking in the (*A very explosive "p-palace" right into* SIMON'S *face.*) palace of sin. (*He beats his breast, and wails.*) Wretch that I am, (*Beats his breast and hides head in arm on back of sofa.*) wretch that I am.

VERA. Oh, that's wonderful, Bromley.

BROMLEY. (*Modestly, looking up.*) I done a bit in my time, miss.

SIMON. No need to spit in my eye, Bromley.

BROMLEY. Begging your pardon, sir—it's the palace bit that does it. (*Does the same "palace" again into* SIMON'S *face.*)

(RIGGIE *rises, crosses to* R. *end of sofa between* TONY *and* SIMON. BROMLEY *goes* D. L. *below table, his back to audience in a position of anguish.*)

TONY. Now, it's my entrance. (TONY *takes villain's moustache from pocket, puts it on, picks up his hat from beside* VERA. *He strides across to* D. L. *and, sweeping* BROMLEY *aside, "enters" to* D. L. C.) Out of me way, Hardy. Aha! Aha! so the old lady is dead, is she? He! He! He! He!

JOHN. (*Advancing* L. *below sofa to meet* TONY *at* L. *end of it.*) You dare to invade the sanctity of a sick room!

TONY. Bah! (*Snaps his fingers at* JOHN, *just catching his chin*)

JOHN. Hey! Steady on! (*Retires* R. *to* RIGGIE'S R., *nursing his chin.*)

BROMLEY (*Throwing his arms to heaven.*) I am still in his toils. Is there no escape, no escape? (*Turns away* L. *bowed*)

TONY. Have you told your daughter, Hardy?

BROMLEY (*Kneels at* TONY'S *feet.*) Have pity, Hepplewhite, have pity.

TONY. Spea—

RIGGIE. (*Interrupting.*) I'm hungry!

TONY. (*Turning to* RIGGIE.) Can't you forget your stomach for five minutes! Speak, Hardy.

BROMLEY. (*Rising and turning away* L.) I cannot. I dare not.

TONY. Speak.

SIMON. The dialogue's a bit monotonous.

TONY. Shut up! Then I will tell her, Hardy. (*Crosses* R. *to* RIGGIE, *kisses her hand, his moustache sticks to it,* ALL *laugh.* TONY *sticks it on again and drags* RIGGIE L. *Stands* L. *of her, below table.*) Millie, me girl, your father has consented that you should be me bride.

JOHN. Foul villain, never!

RIGGIE. No, no, a thousand times, no. Can I have an apple?

ALL. No!!

BROMLEY. Alas, what can I do?

JOHN. (*A step to audience in a heavy "aside."*) Whilst at Oxford I received my blue for fisticuffs, and know what to do. (*Turns to* TONY, *taking up a pugilistic attitude.*) Unhand that innocent girl, Hepplewhite.

RIGGIE. Help! Help! (ALL *turn the page.*) Help!

JOHN. (*Crosses* L. *to her.*) I am here, my dearest one.

TONY. (*To* RIGGIE.) Out of my way, wench! (*Pushes* RIGGIE U. S. *between sofa and table. To* JOHN.) You mealy-mouthed young pup!

(TONY *and* JOHN *throw scripts down on sofa, do a mock fight,* JOHN *backing to in front of sofa.* BROMLEY *sings "hurry" music, while* VERA *runs to piano and plays.* RIGGIE *returns to* D. L. *corner of sofa.* BROMLEY *hurls himself on* SIMON, *weeping—really playing his part.* SIMON *struggles to get free. He and* BROMLEY *roll to the floor knocking over* TONY *and* JOHN. TONY *catches on to* RIGGIE *to save himself and they both fall on to sofa.* JOHN *falls on top of* SIMON *and* BROMLEY. *In the midst of all this* SIR LANCELOT *enters. He surveys the scene in wonder.*)

VERA. (*To above sofa.*) Get up, it's Sir Lancelot.

(JOHN *retreats* L. *to* L. *side of table*, BROMLEY *crawls on all fours round* L. *side of sofa, and hides behind it.* TONY *and* RIGGIE *get to their feet*, TONY *on* RIGGIE'S L. *at* L. *end of sofa.* SIMON *unaware of* SIR LANCELOT'S *presence crawls towards him below armchair muttering. Stops dead at* SIR LANCELOT'S *feet and gets up to face him, hoisting his "bosom"*)

SIMON. Good evening, sir. (*Takes off nightcap, throws it in armchair.* TONY *puts top hat on sofa arm.*)

SIR LANCELOT. *Good* evening. *Good* evening. You have the impertinence to stand there in your nightshirt and bid me good evening.

SIMON. It's not *my* nightshirt, sir.

SIR LANCELOT. Don't mutter, boy. Speak up.

SIMON. We were rehearsing, sir, (*Turning towards the others.*) for the Christmas show.

SIR LANCELOT. Don't lie to me. You were brawling, boy. Brawling. (*To* RIGGIE.) I've seen you before.

(TONY *goes up to the piano, gets an apple from bowl on piano and returns to below* L. *end of sofa.*)

RIGGIE. Yes, sir. I mean, no, sir.

(SIR LANCELOT *crosses below* SIMON *to* R. *of* RIGGIE, *points his stick at her bottom.*)

SIR LANCELOT. I never forget a face. Have I operated on you lately?

RIGGIE No, sir.

(VERA *goes up to drinks cabinet and pours a glass of sherry.* BROMLEY *crawls from behind sofa to divan.* VERA *helps him on with his coat.*)

SIR LANCELOT. I thought so. Well, you look all right

now. But you should take things more quietly. Can't expect to get better in this atmosphere.

RIGGIE. But you didn't . . .

TONY. (*Puts apple in* RIGGIE'S *mouth to stop her talking.*) Never mind, Riggie.

(RIGGIE *goes between* SIR LANCELOT *and the sofa, up* R. *side of it, to behind it.*)

SIR LANCELOT. Grimsdyke—I might have known it. Look at you all! Prospective doctors! God help the patients of tomorrow, that is all I can say. The undertakers will be working overtime. (*To* SIMON.) You, boy—pay attention. And take that damned shroud off. (SIR LANCELOT *hits* SIMON'S *bosom with his cane, cushion falls out,* SIMON *picks it up, puts it in armchair, goes up* L *of armchair.* BROMLEY *comes down* R. *of armchair, and surreptitiously opens the door.* SIMON *takes off nightdress, puts it on divan, and sits on divan.* SIR LANCELOT *takes off hat and puts it on armchair, gloves too, notices* BROMLEY *escaping*) Where are you going?

BROMLEY. (*Closes door, turns to face* SIR LANCELOT) Me, sir? Nowhere, sir.

SIR LANCELOT. Then don't creep, man. I hate creepers. Where have I seen you before?

BROMLEY. (*A step to* SIR LANCELOT.) At the hospital, sir.

SIR LANCELOT. That's it. Never forget a face. You're that new house-surgeon in Casualty. Right?

BROMLEY. Well, sir . . .

(JOHN *moves up to above table, gets his jacket from the chair, puts it on, puts his straw hat on chair by corner cupboard* U. L.)

SIR LANCELOT. Oh, don't prevaricate, man. I know, you see. And let me tell you, as an older man you should know better than to encourage these young whips in their blasted tomfoolery.

VERA (*Coming down to his* R. *with a glass of sherry.*) Can I offer you a drink, Sir Lancelot?

(BROMLEY *goes up to divan, takes his coat off, puts it on divan.*)

SIR LANCELOT. Thank you. What is it?
VERA. Sherry.
SIR LANCELOT. Mm. Wouldn't put it past you to poison me. Did have a student try it once. Still, we'll risk it. As for you, young lady, I advise you to make yourself scarce. The matron is down below in my car, and if she should take it into her head to come up here, your nursing career will come to an abrupt end.

(*General panic.* SIMON *rises, tells* BROMLEY *to get* RIGGIE'S *things from chair below door* D. R. *He does so, hands them to* SIMON. JOHN *comes to* RIGGIE'S L. *behind sofa.* TONY *kneels on sofa. All are talking.* BROMLEY *returns to door* D. R. *keeping guard.* SIMON *to* RIGGIE'S R. *behind sofa.*)

VERA. (*Shouting above the din.*) I'm not a nurse. Thank you all the same. (*Behind sofa to* R. *of group.*)

(*They are all shouting advice to* RIGGIE *at once, crowding round her.*)

SIR LANCELOT. (*Shouting, goes to* R. *side of sofa.*) Stop that muttering. (*It stops.*) Now, get the girls into the bedroom out of the way.
SIMON. Yes, sir. Vera, do you mind? (*Gives clothes to* RIGGIE.)

(TONY *rises, stands in front of sofa.* BROMLEY *straightens armchair to face* D. S., *puts tray and spoon on divan, comes down to* D. R. *of armchair.* VERA *takes* RIGGIE *into the bedroom* U. R. SIR LANCELOT *drinks his sherry and hands the glass to* JOHN *who puts it on the piano and comes back to above sofa,* L. *end.*)

SIR LANCELOT. Well, we've tasted worse sherry. (*Coming down between sofa and armchair facing* TONY.) Now, which of you specimens is me nephew, eh?

SIMON. (*Coming down to* R. *of* SIR LANCELOT.) I am, sir.

SIR LANCELOT. (*Turns to face* SIMON.) Why the devil haven't you written to your parents, eh?

SIMON. I wrote last month, sir.

SIR LANCELOT. Your father is worried. He doesn't hear enough from you. So he writes to me for a report, as though I haven't got enough to do. Are you learning anything?

SIMON. I think so, sir.

SIR LANCELOT. Well, aren't you certain, boy? What are you on now?

SIMON. I've just started on surgery, sir.

SIR LANCELOT. Surgery, eh? Well, we'll just have a little test. (*Hands his stick to* SIMON, *takes off his coat,* BROMLEY *steps in to take it.* SIR LANCELOT *gives coat to* SIMON *who goes above armchair putting coat and stick on it.* SIR LANCELOT *and* BROMLEY *are below armchair. To* BROMLEY.) You, doctor. You can be the guinea-pig.

BROMLEY. Guinea-pig, sir?

SIR LANCELOT Naturally. I'm going to put these boys through their paces. I shall need a body. You can be it.

BROMLEY. (*Tries to go to door.*) I ought to go to my aunt, sir. She's very sick . . .

SIR LANCELOT. (*Pulls* BROMLEY *back by catching hem of his jacket.*) Your aunt can wait. This is in the interests of medicine, doctor.

BROMLEY. I'd better come clean, sir. I'm not a doctor . . .

SIR LANCELOT. Don't mutter. Hate mutterers. (*To* U. R *end of sofa To* JOHN.) Clear that table, boy. (JOHN *opens a curtain of* D. S *window, clears tray of mugs, to*

DOCTOR IN THE HOUSE

window seat, then microscope and scripts, pulls out pouffe, to D. R. *of table.*) Now we'll see how much you've learned . . . (*Comes down again to* L. *of* BROMLEY, *brings him below* R. *of sofa*) You, doctor, get on the table . . .

BROMLEY. I'm not a doctor.

SIR LANCELOT. Lying to me, eh? I suppose you know the penalty for posing as a man of medicine? (*Pushes* BROMLEY L. BROMLEY *goes below table.* SIR LANCELOT *crosses* L) Take your jacket off. Get on that table. (*Turning to face* SIMON *at* D. R. *corner of table.* SIMON *crosses above sofa to* L. *end, indicating door* U. L.) Where's your bathroom, boy? Got to wash my hands.

SIMON. In there, sir!

SIR LANCELOT. Right! (*He goes off into the bedroom* U. L.)

BROMLEY. I'm going . . . (*Runs* R. TONY *stops him.* JOHN *grabs his* L. *arm, they propel him to below pouffe.* SIMON *pulls table about a foot to the* L. *over the stool.*)

TONY. No you don't. We've got to humour the old boy. (TONY *gets* BROMLEY'S *jacket off.* JOHN *gets his tie off.*)

JOHN. I told you he was a bloody butcher . . .

BROMLEY. He ain't going to cut me open. I'm sensitive. I bleed easy.

TONY. We won't let him hurt you.

JOHN. Much.

BROMLEY. If he mentions blood, I'm a goner. Can't stand it.

TONY. You're a hospital porter. You've seen gallons of the stuff.

(*They force him down on to pouffe.*)

BROMLEY. That's different. It wasn't my blood.

SIMON. (*At* R. *side of table.*) I think he's crackers.

BROMLEY. I would do a lot for you young gentlemen, (*He rises and runs* L. TONY *and* JOHN *go after him, and stop him.*) but I have to see a man about a pedigree

pup . . . (*He is heading for the door, when* SIR LANCE-
LOT *appears. He carries his jacket over his arm, and is
wiping his hands on a towel.* SIMON *crosses to* L. *of table.*
SIR LANCELOT *puts his jacket on the back of the sofa.*)

SIR LANCELOT. All ready. Damn it, where's the body?
(TONY *and* JOHN *restrain* BROMLEY *and carry him,
struggling slightly, over to the table.*) You take as long
as this in the hospital the patient'll be dead . . . Lay
him out—take off his shirt . . . And look sharp about
it—I haven't got all night . . . (*They sit* BROMLEY *on
front of table, and take off his shirt. He folds his arms,
embarrassed.* SIMON *puts the chair from* L. *of table to
below table for* BROMLEY'S *feet, goes to top* L. *of table.*
JOHN *goes up to* L. *of table.* TONY *takes* BROMLEY'S
shirt and jacket which he has still on his arm to D. S.
window, puts them on window seat. Stands below JOHN.
Comes to R. *of table, puts the towel under* BROMLEY'S
head as a pillow.) Right. (*To* BROMLEY.) Now you just
lie still and keep quiet. Don't you take any notice of
what I'm going to say to these young doctors. (*Pum-
melling* BROMLEY'S *middle.*) Now, what's this?

BROMLEY. Me spare tyre, sir . . .

SIR LANCELOT. We'll soon puncture that, eh? (*He roars
at his joke, then notices* SIMON *and the others standing
well back.*) Come over here! How often have I got to
tell you young fellers you can't learn surgery from the
door-post? (*They gather round.*) Now, for our purposes,
this is a hospital and this is our patient. I'm going to
find out just what you do know. (*To* SIMON.) Take a
look at that abdomen. (SIMON *steps forward and
twitches here and there. There is a squeal from* BROM-
LEY.) Take your dirty little hands away, sir! (*He flicks*
SIMON'S *hand away.*) The first rule of surgery, gentlemen Eyes first and most, hands next and least, tongue
not at all. Look first and don't chatter. (*Starts to undo
top of* BROMLEY'S *trousers.* BROMLEY *protests.*) And you,
damn you, lie still, or I'll carve you with a blasted fish-
slice. Come on, you other chaps—you're in it, too. Have

a look. (TONY *bends his head close to* BROMLEY'S *stomach which rises and falls as he breathes.* TONY'S *head follows the motion*) Well, what do you think?

TONY. (*Turns away to window.*) Horrible.

SIR LANCELOT. Now—feel him . . . feel him.

TONY. Me, sir?

SIR LANCELOT. Yes, yes—go on. (TONY *returns to* BROMLEY, *slaps both hands heavily on* BROMLEY'S *middle.* SIR LANCELOT *pushes him away.*) *Doucemong, doucemong*—gently boy, you're not making bread. What am I always telling you a successful surgeon must have? (*Points to* TONY.)

TONY. The eye of a hawk . . . (*To* JOHN.)

JOHN. The heart of a lion . . . (*To* SIMON.)

SIMON And the hand of a lady . . .

SIR LANCELOT. Ah—you do listen. That's something.

TONY (*Turning away, mutters.*) No other choice . . .

SIR LANCELOT. What?

TONY. (*Turning back.*) Nothing, sir . . .

SIR LANCELOT. Then don't mumble. Hate mumblers. Right—to our patient. We have examined him. What do we find?

SIMON. (*Leaning over* BROMLEY *from top of table, feeling his diaphragm*) Well, actually, sir—there is something a bit funny here . . .

SIR LANCELOT. A bit funny? Do you imagine that is the language of a surgeon? What's funny?

(SIMON *having stood up,* TONY *now bends over* BROMLEY *feeling him.*)

TONY. There's a lump here, sir—tucked under the edge of the ribs—about the size of a large walnut, sir.

SIR LANCELOT Now that is interesting . . . (*He feels* BROMLEY'S *middle* BROMLEY *grunts in pain*) You're quite right. Good lad. (*To* BROMLEY) How long have you had that, doctor?

BROMLEY. (*Sitting up*) Had what?

SIR LANCELOT. This. Feel it, man, feel it.

BROMLEY. (*Feeling it.*) Oh, that. That's me lump. I've always had it.

SIR LANCELOT Good God! It's a wonder you're alive. You're a surgeon and you didn't even bother to have it out?

BROMLEY. I like it. It's no bother.

SIR LANCELOT. It's got no business to be there. And it's not going to remain there It is coming out.

BROMLEY. It doesn't hurt. And I wouldn't feel the same without it, sir. (BROMLEY *stands on the chair below table.* TONY *and* SIR LANCELOT *grab him.*) Please, sir . . .

SIR LANCELOT (*Pushing him down.*) Oh, lie back and stop whimpering. (JOHN, *interested in the lump, leans on* BROMLEY's *middle.*) Now, gentlemen, it seems as though—by a fortunate accident—we have come across a real case. (*To* JOHN, *pushing him off.*) Don't lean on the patient, boy. If I'm not tired you shouldn't be, and I can give you twenty or thirty years . . .

BROMLEY. (*Sitting up.*) Could I put me shirt on now? I feel awfully chilly.

SIR LANCELOT. (*Pushing him down.*) Lie down, man. We're trying to save your life and all you can think about is your blasted shirt! (*To* JOHN.) *You*—see if you can summon the energy to step downstairs to my car and ask the Matron to come up here.

(TONY *and* SIMON *confer behind* JOHN's *back.*)

JOHN. Here, sir?

SIR LANCELOT. Here? Of course, here? Where else? I want her to phone the hospital. This man needs immediate attention, and he shall have it.

TONY. If you don't mind, sir . . . couldn't we leave it until tomorrow?

(MATRON *enters.*)

ACT II   DOCTOR IN THE HOUSE   79

SIR LANCELOT. Why do all students have to argue with their betters? Get the Matron, man.

(BROMLEY *hurriedly takes the towel from his head and covers his face with it. The three boys turn in together by the* U. S. *window.*)

MATRON. There is no need. I am here already.

(*They turn to find her standing at the door. She is, to put it briefly, a fine body of a woman. She was not born so much as quarried. She looks at the students with ineffable contempt as she comes in at* SIR LANCELOT'S *invitation.*)

SIR LANCELOT. Ah—come here, Matron. I want you to feel this . . . (SIR LANCELOT *goes to the top of the table.* MATRON *comes to* R. *of table.*)

MATRON. May I ask what is going on here, Sir Lancelot? We have a meeting at the hospital in fifteen minutes and . . .

SIR LANCELOT. It can wait. Quite by accident we have stumbled on a most interesting case. I was just using this doctor here as a guinea-pig to test our young friends in their knowledge of elementary surgery when this lump turned up.

MATRON. (*Sweeps the towel off* BROMLEY'S *face.*) Doctor? This is Bromley, one of the hospital porters. What are you doing here, may I ask?

SIR LANCELOT. Damn it, what the hell does it matter what he's doing here? The fact is, he's got a lump.

MATRON. There is no need to swear, Sir Lancelot. (SIR LANCELOT *walks away* R. *in disgust. To* TONY.) I know you. You're the young man who is always interfering with the nurses.

TONY Oh no, ma'am.

SIR LANCELOT. (*Returning to top of table.*) Oh, for heaven's sake, Matron, I didn't bring you up here to give a lecture on sex. I've a case here. I want you to reserve a bed—I shall operate as soon as possible.

BROMLEY. No!

SIR LANCELOT. Don't worry, man. You're not in the hands of one of these modern specialists. I shan't fiddle with you. Matron, feel this lump . . .

(MATRON *does so.* BROMLEY *jumps and sits up.*)

BROMLEY. Ow! Your hands are cold.

MATRON. Don't be impertinent. How long has this been here?

BROMLEY. Thirty years.

MATRON. Then you should have had the decency to tell us before. Sir Lancelot is a busy man. (BROMLEY *lies down again. To* SIR LANCELOT.) I can arrange for one of the other surgeons to fit this in, Sir Lancelot . . .

SIR LANCELOT. Nonsense. I intend to do it myself—and these young fellers shall watch me in the act. (MATRON *breaks a little* R. SIR LANCELOT *comes to* R. *of table.*) Now—we'll assume we have gone through the routine. We know where the lump is, and what it is . . . Where are we going to make the incision, eh?

BROMLEY. Please . . .

SIR LANCELOT. Nearly finished with you, my man. (*Taking grease pencil out of his waistcoat pocket.*) Here boy, use this pencil. (*Hands pencil to* SIMON.)

SIMON. Here, sir? (*He draws a modest line over the lesion.*)

SIR LANCELOT. Keyhole surgery! Damnable! Give me that pencil! (*He takes the red grease-pencil from* SIMON *and draws a broad, decisive sweep on* BROMLEY'S *flesh.*) Here—and here! (*Raises* BROMLEY *up.*) This, gentlemen, will be our incision! We will open the patient like *that*. (*Describes a large opening with his hand. Pushes* BROMLEY *down again.*) Then we can have a good look inside. It's no good rummaging around an abdomen if you can't get your hand in properly. What do we do then, eh? Do you think it's going to be easy to remove?

JOHN. Er . . . No, sir?

SIR LANCELOT. Quite right—it's going to be most difficult. There are at least a dozen ways in which we can make a slight error and kill the patient like that! (BROMLEY *groans.*) Don't worry, doctor, we haven't started yet! Now . . . When we have cut through the skin, gentlemen, what is the next structure we shall meet? Come along, come along. You've done your anatomy more recently than I have. What do we meet next?

SIMON. Subcutaneous fat, sir?

SIR LANCELOT. (*Patting* SIMON's *shoulder*) Excellent—excellent. Yes, subcutaneous fat. Then, gentlemen, we encounter the surgeon's worst enemy. What is that? For heaven's sake, don't you boys learn anything? What do we meet next? I'll tell you—blood, gentlemen—B—L—O—O—D! (*With a groan* BROMLEY *rolls from the table to* R. *of it—out cold.* SIR LANCELOT *steps back. The three boys crowd round* BROMLEY. TONY *on his* L. JOHN *steps over to his feet, and kneels on his* R. SIMON *above him.* SIR LANCELOT *goes above* L. *end of sofa.*) Oh, well, that will do for today, gentlemen. But tomorrow—we shall really get to work . . .

(*The noise of* BROMLEY's *fall brings* VERA *and* RIGGIE *hurrying in.* RIGGIE, *seeing* MATRON, *rushes to door* D. R. MATRON *crosses below sofa. Three boys crouch behind* L. *end of sofa hiding.*)

VERA. (*Coming to above sofa.*) What on earth is the matter?

MATRON. (*Like thunder, to* RIGGIE.) And what are you doing here, Nurse Winslow?

RIGGIE. Matron . . . I . . .

MATRON Don't tell me! I know only too well. You will be in my office at nine a.m. tomorrow. (*Sweeping round on the others. Three boys rise.* JOHN *to* L. *of* SIMON, TONY *to* L. *of* JOHN.) As for you! The Dean shall hear of this—and—*and* if any of you—any one of you—are at St. Swithin's in a week's time, I shall be extremely surprised! (*Escorts the bewildered* RIGGIE *through the door.*)

(SIMON *to* R. *of table,* TONY *to* L. *of it,* JOHN *above.*)

SIR LANCELOT. Wonderful woman, that. Bags of drive. (SIR LANCELOT *picks up jacket and starts to put it on.*) I remember when she laid old Rollo Foote flat on his back for raising an eyebrow at a nurse. Used a bed-pan on him. (BROMLEY *groans and props himself up against the arm of the sofa.* SIR LANCELOT *puts jacket down again.*) Oh, nearly forgotten about you, hadn't we, doctor? (*Coming down a step* R. *of sofa.* JOHN *sits on table above it.* SIMON *sits* R. *side. They look very glum.*) Well, gentlemen, shall we continue? After we've cut through the subcutaneous fat, the patient is going to bleed. Well, we can't help that, that's what we're here for. (JOHN *and* SIMON *whisper together.*) Fortunately, after a certain period, the chemicals in the blood stream form a clot and stop it. Now, this interval is known scientifically as the bleeding-time. (*To* SIMON, *who is whispering to* JOHN.) You, boy, what's the bleeding-time? (*Slapping* SIMON'S *arm.*)

SIMON. (*Coming to with a start and looking at his watch.*) Half-past six, sir.

(SIR LANCELOT *turns away in disgust while* JOHN *and* TONY *tell* SIMON *what a clot he is.*)

CURTAIN

PROLOGUE TO ACT THREE

TONY GRIMSDYKE *appears before the curtain, as before.*

TONY. Still with us? Good show. Well, we now shove the old clock on a couple of years. The Matron? Well, we squeezed out of our last little difficulty quite nicely—thanks to a bit of backstage manoeuvring from old Sir Lancelot. But ever since then the old cabbage has had her knife into us—with a special cutting edge reserved for poor old Simon. If a nurse raises an eyebrow at him in the hospital—she's fired forthwith. From the remarks the Matron made when she caught Simon applying a cold-water compress to a probationer's ankle, you'd have thought they'd just spent a naughty week-end in Brighton. Shame, really, because old Simon works damned hard. Unfortunately, he still gets these outbreaks of *orchitis amorosa acuta*—we did explain, madam, but if you didn't hear, that is the professional term for the normal, human desire to love and be loved. He gets these outbreaks of mooniness, about twice a month during the spring and summer— Now, alas, it is nearly spring. Simon is in the mood, as they say. The old Matron is watching him like a hawk. And—with a wonderful sense of timing—Janet enters the lists. (*He moves to depart, then—as though remembering something—turns again to the audience.*) Janet? My apologies, profound and humble, for introducing another female so late in our entertainment. Against all the rules, I know. But necessity and all that . . . Anyway—see for yourselves . . . (*He disappears. After a moment or two the curtain rises on Act Three.*)

ACT THREE

SCENE 1

Several new signs have now appeared. The skeleton is no longer in evidence. The lights are on. The curtains are open, windows closed. The sofa table has gone, the big table is in its original position, the stool is against the wall, between the mirrors, the chair from the side of the table is now in the bedroom U. L. The sofa at the moment is straight up and down stage facing the table, the armchair is six inches more U. S. than before. The rug is rolled up on the sofa. Pouffe is below D. R. corner of table. VERA is arranging the room, using JOHN as furniture shifter. JOHN is D. R. C. having just put the sofa in position. He is smoking a very large pipe. VERA is below the armchair D. R.

VERA. Let me see, John, put the lamp there, (*Indicating the table.* JOHN *goes up to the corner cupboard and moves the lamp to the table.*) and leave the table there—for drinks . . .

JOHN. Right. You haven't seen old Simon's latest wench, have you? The one that's coming tonight?

VERA. I have not. But I think he's mad. With the finals so near—and the Matron on his trail—crazy . . .

JOHN. (*Coming to L. of the U. S. sofa arm.*) It's the element of adventure which puts spice into life, dear girl.

TONY. (*Enters briskly from bedroom U. R., to R. of* JOHN.) How are we doing? Good heavens—who arranged the couch like this?

VERA. I did. What's wrong?

TONY. Vera, my pigeon, you're slipping. Simon wants to seduce her—not show her his snapshots.

VERA. Don't be crude.

TONY. (*Moving couch.*) Lend a hand, John. (*He pulls the* D. S. *end of the sofa* R. JOHN *pushes the* U. S. *end* D. R. *so that the sofa is much squarer on to the audience than in Act I.* JOHN *stands above* L. *of sofa.* TONY *comes to his* R.) Here—this is the place. And that table must be within hand's reach. I ruined a wonderful opportunity once because the table with the drinks was too far away.

VERA. (*Coldly.*) Very interesting.

TONY. (*Sits* R. *end of sofa.*) Point is, you more or less get yourself set for the spring. Maybe you've got your arm round the girl— (*Picking up a cushion and embracing it.*) she's already beginning to melt a little—then you want to pour her another drink and you find you've got to get up to do it! (*Dropping the cushion he rises, demonstrating and crosses below table to* L. *of it.*) You can wreck an hour's spadework that way. Give me a hand with the table, John.

(*They move to the table close in to the sofa.* TONY *pushing,* JOHN *pulling, they bring it close to the sofa, the* D. S *edge next to the* L. *arm of sofa, and parallel to the footlights.*)

VERA. (*Crosses to armchair* D. R.) You should write a handbook.

TONY. Now don't get mad, my pigeon. (*Crosses to* VERA. JOHN *gets a paper out from behind* L. *sofa cushion.*) You wouldn't have liked me half so much had I come to you with the dew of innocence still damp on my brow. Experience is a valuable asset, and most intelligent women realize it.

VERA. (*Sits on* L. *arm of armchair.*) Tony, you're disgusting, absolutely disgusting. If I didn't know you . . .

TONY. But you do. (*Bending over* VERA, *he puts his arm round her.*) And you know that underneath all this filthy exterior there beats a pure and contrite heart. (*Kisses her. To* R. *of sofa.*) Now, let me see. Drink is arranged?

JOHN. Half a bottle of gin. (*He puts his paper on the table. Goes to the drinks cabinet and brings two glasses, a half bottle of gin and a bottle of orange squash which he puts on the* U. S. *side of the table, picks up his paper.*)

TONY. (*Looking at the rug rolled up on the sofa.*) This isn't very tidy. (*He lays it in front of the sofa.*) Half a bottle of gin, eh?

JOHN. Uh-huh.

(TONY *crosses* L., *draws the curtains* U. S. *then* D. S. *Pushes the wooden armchair, which was above the table* L., *towards the stool facing* D. R.)

TONY. Not the most liberal of arrangements, but all we could afford. You know, I feel positively paternal. Simon always brings that out in me.

JOHN (*Climbing over the sofa arm to in front of it.*) You know he's had some rotten luck lately. And I'm not at all sure about this new nurse—the one that's coming tonight. I think he'll find her more of a handful. (*He sits on the* D. S. *end of the sofa, putting his feet up.*) Pity old Rigor Mortis ain't still around.

TONY. She's doing awfully well. (*Sits on the pouffe.*) Married that undertaker feller who was courting her.

(JOHN *buries himself in his paper, and* SIMON *enters from the bedrooom* U. L. *brandishing a tie. He comes down to* TONY'S L.)

SIMON. Tony, old boy, lend me a decent tie. Some clot has spilled gravy all down this one.

TONY. A tie? What the devil do you want a tie for? You're not going out anywhere.

SIMON. (*Nudging him.*) I'm entertaining a lady!

TONY. This is the twentieth century, old boy. The emphasis is on casual wear. Sweater, sports shirt, flannel bags, that's the thing. Gives you that man-of-the-world atmosphere, with a touch of the healthy, tweedy, virile type thrown in. Can't miss.

(SIMON *goes up to the* L. *side of the table. Puts his tie down on it and takes a cravat out of his pocket.*)

VERA. (*Slipping into the seat of the armchair.*) You wear a tie if you want to, Simon.

(SIMON *crosses to the mirror between the two windows.*)

TONY. He doesn't *need* to. Dammit, who's organizing this affair? She's not coming here because she wants to see the colour of his old school tie!

VERA. Don't shout!

TONY. (*Shouting.*) I am *not* shouting!

VERA. (*Very calmly.*) Then lower your voice!

TONY. (*Rises and crosses* R. *towards* VERA.) My dear girl, I am merely trying to assist my good friend Simon in his arrangements for this evening. (*Crosses* L. *to* R. *of* SIMON.) Of course, if Simon doesn't want the benefit of my accumulated experience . . .

SIMON. (*Who is looking in the mirror adjusting his cravat.*) I think I'll wear a cravat, just something round the neck, you know. (*Sits on the* L. *arm of the armchair by mirror.*) I've got rather a prominent Adam's apple which tends to swell when I get excited, and Janet's a very tidy person. (*Sits properly in his chair.*)

VERA. (*Rising.*) I've a jolly good mind to go downstairs and warn this poor little innocent girl. You're like a lot of spiders—waiting here in your web.

TONY. (*Crosses* R. *to* VERA *and turns her* U. S. *towards the door* U. R.) Look—we've got to scarper before she arrives. Go and powder your nose, pigeon, and leave the men to their work. (*Pats* VERA'S *behind to push her* U. S.)

VERA (*Pausing.*) Have you told them yet, Tony? (*She comes back to behind* TONY'S R. *shoulder.*)

TONY. (*Purposely not understanding.*) Told them what, pigeon?

VERA. (*Taking his arm.*) About us.

TONY. (*Looking at* JOHN *and* SIMON.) Oh, I think they know. I mean—we've pretty open and carefree about everything . . .

VERA. You know exactly what I mean.

TONY. Oh. Oh, yes. About . . . about the other. (*He escapes* L. *along the back of the sofa*) I will tell 'em, love. When I get a minute.

VERA. (*Pulls* TONY *back to her.*) You are wriggling again. Until you *do* tell them, I shan't believe you.

JOHN. (*Moves along to* L. *of sofa, faces them.*) What is this double-talk?

TONY. (*A deep breath.*) Well, old boy, fact is that Vera has asked me to marry her—and I have consented.

VERA. Oooh . . . you beast. (*Pummels* TONY'S *back with her fists.*)

SIMON. (*Crosses.*) I say, that's marvelous.

TONY. (*Unenthusiastically.*) Yes.

VERA. (*Pulls* TONY *down by his ear, to in front of sofa, she stands* R. *of it*) He's so enthusiastic, you see. Tell them when it's going to be, sweetie. (*Kicks at him.*)

SIMON. Yes, when's the wedding going to be?

TONY. As soon as I've passed my finals.

JOHN. Supposing you don't pass?

TONY. (*Cheerfully.*) That throws the whole question open once more. (*Crosses to center of sofa, sits next to* JOHN.)

VERA. He is going to pass.

SIMON. (*Crosses* R. *to* VERA *at* R. *of sofa.*) I'm sure of it. His work has bucked up no end.

TONY. My friend. (*Grabs* SIMON'S *hand over sofa arm.* SIMON *turns to him. To* VERA.) Look, pigeon—this isn't our show. It's Simon's . . . go and get ready.

VERA. Poor Tony. (*Coming to behind* TONY, *leaning over him. He leans his head back.*) He looks like a captured cow. But I don't care. I know what is best for you, you see, and I don't intend to back out now. *Voilà!* (*Kisses his lips, bending over him.*) Give him a drop of your gin, Simon . . . just to cheer him. (*Exits* U R.)

SIMON Do you want a drink, Tony? (*Sits* R. *of sofa next to* TONY.)

TONY. No, thanks. One wouldn't be enough.

JOHN. Vera's a wonder, old boy. Don't you want to marry her?

TONY. If I've *got* to marry, then she's the only one. But hang it—I'm one of nature's bachelors—I was born to be foot-loose and fancy-free.

SIMON. But you don't have to marry her, surely.

TONY. If I don't, she'll leave me flat. And I know that if she does, Grimsdyke will be an almighty flop. Personally, I'd like to go on just as we are—but Vera says the children wouldn't like it.

JOHN. What children?

TONY. The one Vera intends to produce after the finals. Two girls and two boys—in six years. She's got it planned down to the last safety-pin.

SIMON. Well, I wish you joy, Tony. I know one thing—I'm not getting married for years and years. Too much to do.

JOHN. I don't know. I wouldn't mind marrying a girl like Vera.

TONY. It wouldn't work—I'd hate having you in the house all the time. (*Rises, crosses to behind* SIMON'S R. *shoulder*) No. I guess I'll take my medicine. Now are you all set, Simon?

SIMON. I think so.

TONY. We can leave you to it?

SIMON. I wish you didn't have to.

TONY. There'd be too much of a crush on the couch if we stayed, old boy.

JOHN. There are some situations, Simon, which a man must handle in his own way. Women are most of them.

SIMON. I feel such a clot. Always dry up at the crucial moment—tongue sticks to the roof of my mouth—and I know I look like a blasted goldfish. (*Opens and shuts his mouth*)

TONY. You've got an inferiority complex about women, old chap Next time you look at one—just remember that they wouldn't be here at all if Adam hadn't given up one of his ribs.

JOHN I might be something in your past, y'know. Did you ever have a baby-sitter who burned your favourite teddy-bear? That sort of thing leaves a scar.

(TONY *laughs.*)

SIMON. I'm serious.

TONY. Listen, chum, I'll give you a tip. Women—all women—love to be flattered.

SIMON Janet says she hates flattery.

TONY. Which means she loves it. Turn it full on, old boy. (*Gestures towards him with clenched fist.* SIMON *copies him.*) Whenever you feel stuck for a line tell her something corny about her eyes.

SIMON. Like what?

TONY. Blimey, he wants me to write the blessed dialogue as well. (*Crosses* R. *a little*) Use your imagination! Above all—be sweeping. Exaggerate.

JOHN The big lie technique, Simon.

TONY. (*Crosses to in front of armchair* D. R.) She hasn't got the loveliest blue eyes in London—they're the lovelist blue eye in the entire universe.

SIMON. (*Rises.*) She hasn't got blue eyes. They're brown, I think. (*Sits* R *arm of sofa*)

TONY. What can you do with him? (*Collapses in armchair, hands raised in despair*)

JOHN. (*Rises. A step to* SIMON.) Tell her she's different, old chap. You don't have to qualify it. Everyone likes to feel they're different.

TONY. And that she's intelligent. Nothing tickles a woman's fancy so much as the thought that she has brains.

SIMON. But she has. She's frightfully intelligent—cultured and all that.

JOHN I was afraid of that.

TONY. (*Rises, crosses to* R. *arm of sofa*) Sweep it all aside, my lad. She is a woman, too. Flog the old gin and she won't worry about Beethoven. (*A knock at the door.*) Aha.

SIMON. (*Desperate.*) Look—I know I'll make a muck of it . . .

> (TONY *and* JOHN *pull* SIMON *to his feet.*)

TONY. What rot! Open up them golden gates, my boy. You are about to live!

> (TONY *and* JOHN *push him to the door. He looks pleadingly at them. Then turns to door.* SIMON *opens the door to admit* JANET. *She is an attractive girl of about twenty-one. She wears glasses, and she might be described as brisk: yes,* JANET *is brisk.*)

SIMON. Why, Janet—it's you!
JANET. Naturally it's me. You invited me here.
SIMON. That's right—so I did. Well—
TONY. (*The breezy host.*) Don't leave her standing there, Simon. Wheel her in . . . (SIMON *passes* JANET *to his* L., *closes the door, comes to* JANET'S L.) You know me, Janet, of course . . .
JANET. (*Not warmly.*) I do.
TONY. And Johnnie Evans.
JANET. Yes . . .
TONY. Don't worry, old girl. We're just buzzing off.
JOHN. Don't want to get in the way.
JANET. In the way of what?

> (*Laugh between* TONY *and* JOHN. TONY *turns to* JANET, *her blank expression freezes the laugh.*)

TONY. Exactly . . . (*Crossing to bedroom* U. R.) Come on, Vera . . . get your skates on . . .
SIMON. (*Comes to* R. *of armchair.*) Won't you sit down, Janet?
JANET. Thank you . . .

> (*There is a little silence.* JOHN *moves round corner of sofa to behind it.* TONY *comes down to* R. *of* JOHN.)

TONY. Raining?
JANET. No.
JOHN. Looks as though it might.
TONY. Might what?
JOHN. Rain.
TONY. Oh, yes . . . (*Goes up to* VERA *shouting at her as she suddenly enters.*) For Pete's sake, Vera, you take more blasted time to . . . (*Checks himself. Very charmingly. Brings her down on his* R. *to* L. *of armchair.*) Ready, darling? Do you know Janet?
VERA. How do you do? (*Extends her hand to* JANET *who coldly shakes the tip.* SIMON *goes behind armchair.*) So glad you could come.
JANET. Thank you.

(JOHN *taps* TONY *on shoulder, crosses in front of* JANET, *opens door. Holds it open standing above it.*)

VERA. Simon has been telling me all about you.

(TONY *pushes* VERA *to door. They turn in doorway to face* JANET.)

TONY. Well—can't stop. Got an important date. Come on, old girl . . . Bye, Simon—good hunting . . . Well . . . I mean—enjoy yourselves . . .
JOHN. So long . . .
VERA. If you want anything . . .
TONY. If he wants anything he'll get it, won't you, Simon . . . Come on . . . (*And he more or less shoves* VERA *out.* JOHN *follows them, turns off the light switch extinguishing the ceiling light and standard lamp, leaving only the light from the small lamp on the table. He closes the door behind him and their voices die away on the staircase.*)
SIMON. (*Comes round to* JANET'S L., *claps his hands together loudly.*) Well . . . here we are . . .
JANET. Is that—her?

SIMON. Her? Oh, you mean Vera . . . oh yes.
JANET. How she can be *so* brazen . . .
SIMON. Vera?
JANET. You've no need to look so innocent, Simon. I know perfectly well what goes on in this flat. The whole hospital knows.
SIMON. Really?
JANET. I suppose you approve.
SIMON. Er . . . I don't really know.
JANET. Is it true that she comes into the bathroom while you men are in the bath?
SIMON. Oh yes . . . I mean . . . No . . . Well, not very often.
JANET. You needn't try to defend her to me. I'm not narrow-minded, thank heavens, but there is a limit.
SIMON. She is a bit unorthodox, I admit, but she's done wonders for Tony. He'd never've got through his anatomy exams without her. (*Realizes the implication of this and adds hastily*) And they *are* engaged
JANET. (*Scornfully.*) Tony! (*Rises, takes a step* L, *her back to* SIMON, *loosens her coat.* SIMON *takes it off for her*) Honestly, Simon, I don't know why you're so friendly with him. He's not your type, now is he?
SIMON. (*Goes up to divan, puts her coat on it.*) Old Tony? He's the salt of the earth.
JANET. (*Going up to his* L.) You're so simple and so trusting—really, I never met anyone like you. (*He turns to her.*) You need to be taken in hand—you know that?

(*There is a pause.* JANET *moves in to* SIMON, *head on one side, gazing up at him. He tentatively lifts his arms to her, then hurriedly claps them behind his back again.*)

SIMON (*Brightly.*) Have a drink?
JANET Yes, rather. You know, this room is really pathetic.

(SIMON *crosses to above table, pours some orange into*

the two glasses, puts glasses and bottles across table to front of it, walks round to the front. JANET *walks down between armchair and sofa looking round at the room.*)

SIMON. It is a bit of a mess.

JANET. It's juvenile. Now really—admit it. All this junk.

SIMON. (*At front of table.*) I hadn't really noticed.

JANET. (*Crossing to him.*) You wouldn't. (*Tolerantly.*) You live in a dream—an absolute dream . . . (*As he pours drink.*) I say, steady on.

SIMON. (*Puts the bottle down, and gives her a glass, raising his own in a toast.*) Here—bottoms up . . .

JANET. (*Clinks glasses.*) Cheers . . . Here's to us.

SIMON. To us? (*Knocks back his gin and puts the glass down.* JANET *has a sip of hers, then takes it to sofa, sitting* R. *end.*)

JANET. Come and sit by me, Simon, dear—and we'll talk. (SIMON *sits next to her.*) It's so comfy being alone like this. (*A pause.*) Well, haven't you got anything to say to me?

SIMON. (*Does his "goldfish act," mouth open and shut.* SIMON *in a rush.*) Did I tell you about that patient in Prudence Ward? Old Sir Lancelot told me to examine her . . . Before I could start, she told *me* what was wrong . . .

JANET. Really?

SIMON. Yes—came out with it pat: I've got mitral stenosis due to rheumatic fever, but I'm perfectly well compensated and I've a favourable prognosis, she said.

JANET. That's very interesting.

SIMON. Yes, isn't it? But she didn't stop there, oh, dear me no. She told me she had a presystolic murmur at the apex, but that the aortic area was clear and there were no creps at the bases . . . oh, yes, and she said she had a slightly enlarged thyroid, and that she wasn't fibrillating. She knew more about it than I did!

JANET. I'm sure she did . . .

SIMON. You ought to have a look at Charity Ward—No. 9. There's an absolutely top-hole pyelonephritis there—

JANET. Simon . . .

SIMON. (*Moves to* L *of sofa*) Oh, hang it—there I go again.

JANET. You're nervous. I've known you long enough to know that. When you're nervous you always go on about cases in the wards.

SIMON. (*Puts chin in hands, his elbow on* L. *sofa arm.*) Sorry . . .

JANET. *I* don't mind. I shall have to get used to it, won't I?

SIMON. (*Looking up, worried.*) Will you?

JANET. If we're to go on being such close chums—of course. Now—tell me—why are you so nervous?

SIMON. I don't know . . . (*He moves towards her, puts his arm carelessly on the back of the sofa.*)

JANET. Do I make you nervous?

SIMON. No, of course not. (*Plays with his fingers on her* R. *shoulder.*)

JANET. Really, Simon, if you want to put your arm around me, do it. Don't fiddle. (*He removes his arm as though burned and jumps back to* L. *end of sofa A pause, then* JANET *moves up to him and slips down in sofa, her head on back.* SIMON *slides down to her level. Smiling into his eyes.*) I say, you're jolly sweet. D'you know that?

SIMON. (*Coyly.*) Oh, really! (*Leans towards her amorously then says suddenly.*) Would you like another cushion?

JANET. I'm quite comfy, thanks.

SIMON Oh . . . (*He subsides again.*)

JANET. You know, I feel very guilty coming here like this and taking up your time when you should be studying.

SIMON. That's all right.

JANET. (*Sitting up.*) It isn't really. It won't help either of us if you fail now, will it?

SIMON. (*Sitting up.*) Either of us?

JANET. Don't you think I want you to pass? Everyone says you could be a brilliant doctor . . . Look—you get out your books and do some work . . . I'll just curl up here and watch you . . . (*At* R. *end of sofa. Curls her feet up.*)

SIMON. I . . . I don't really feel like it tonight.

JANET. (*A pause. Puts her feet down again.*) Oh, well, what do you feel like?

SIMON. Well, (*A pause. He leans amorously forward to her. She gives a horsey gurgle and he recoils to* L. *end of sofa.*) will you have some more gin . . .

JANET A little then . . . just a spot . . .

SIMON. (*Rising.*) Right . . .

JANET. (*Pulling him down.*) No need to get up It's here—within reach. (*She leans right across him, putting her glass down on the table*) Very thoughtful . . . I'll help myself . . .

SIMON. (*Poking his head forward over her arms, which are on the table. Breathlessly*) You have the most beautiful eyes . . . (*He stops dead.*)

JANET. Yes—go on?

SIMON. Really. Not just beautiful—I mean—stunning . . .

JANET. (*She sits up again, moving* R) As a matter of fact my eyes are one of my worst features. I am very short-sighted. I can hardly see without my glasses . . .

SIMON. What nonsense! You have the most wonderful blue—I mean brown eyes . . . I have . . Did you say short-sighted?

JANET. Yes.

SIMON. (*Really interested now.*) Could I see? I mean . . . I'm going on to eyes soon . . .

JANET. Well—yes . . .

(SIMON *removes her glasses, putting them in his pocket,*

ACT III   DOCTOR IN THE HOUSE

and then begins to examine her R. *eye, holding it open with two fingers.*)

SIMON. Hm . . . I wish I had an ophthalmoscope with me . . . (*Leaning over her.*) The other day I saw a whopping great retinal detachment . . . Have you always been short-sighted?

JANET. Well—yes . . . Could I have my glasses now? (*Groping with her hand.*)

SIMON Just a moment . . . (*Forcing her head right back over the sofa arm.*) hm . . . yes . . . you know, you're just the sort of case I might get in the clinical examination . . .

JANET. Simon—my glasses . . .

SIMON. They're on the table . . .

JANET. (*Rises and crosses to below table, gropes about on it.*) Where?

SIMON. Wait a bit! Old Johnnie Evans has an ophthalmoscope among his kit in the bedroom. (*Rises, crosses in front of her. Goes to bedroom* U. L., *opening the door.*) Come on—might as well take a proper look.

JANET. (*Going up towards door.*) Simon—what are you doing? My glasses . . . Simon!

SIMON. (*Coming down to her* L.) This retinal detachment I saw was . . .

JANET. No! Simon—give me my glasses at once! (*He fumbles in his pocket and brings out the glasses. She puts them on.*) That's better. (*She looks round and sees the open bedroom door. Smiling.*) Simon—I'm surprised at you.

SIMON. Why? What did I do?

JANET. What were you going to do, you naughty boy! (*Gives his shoulder a friendly pummel.*) Is there really an ophthalmoscope in there?

SIMON. Why, yes . . . I think so . . . (*Goes up to door again, switches off light. He closes door, comes down to her* L.) it will only take a minute . . .

JANET. Do you think you can deceive me? (*At* L. *side*

of table. She fiddles with the tie SIMON *left there.*) Do you have to take me in there to look at my eyes?

SIMON. No, of course not. We can do it just as easily out here . . . it was just . . . (*The penny drops.*) Oh, I see—you thought I wanted to . . . I was going to . . .

JANET. (*Archly.*) Weren't you?

SIMON. (*Stoutly.*) Not in *there*. I'd got it all arranged out here. (*Realizing his faux pas he claps a hand to his mouth.*)

JANET. You see? I can read you like a book. (*Brings him down to below table. She sits* R. *end of front edge*, SIMON *sits on her* L.) Don't think I'm offended. I'm not. Just a *leetle* disappointed, that's all. I might have expected it of your friends—but not you, Simon, dear.

SIMON. No?

JANET. You're not really that type, are you now?

SIMON. Doesn't seem so. I can never pull it off.

JANET. (*She straightens his cravat.*) But I'd sooner have you than all the others put together.

SIMON. You would—really?

JANET. Of course. (*Joining her hands on his* R. *shoulder.*) You see, you and I are sensible, serious people. When a thing like this happens to us, we don't want to treat it irresponsibly, do we?

SIMON. Why, no . . . of course not.

JANET. Of course not. (*She rises, pulls him up, takes his* L. *arm and propels him to the sofa.*) You need taking care of, Simon—you need someone who can really look after you . . . permanently. (*Putting both hands on his shoulders she pushes him down on to the* R. *end of the sofa on his* L.) You do love me, Simon?

SIMON. Love?

JANET. I don't mean in the juvenile sense. I mean the love that grows out of mutual respect and friendship. You do respect me, don't you?

SIMON. Yes . . .

JANET. And we are good frends?

SIMON. Of course . . .

JANET. Then—let's face it like adults—you love me.
SIMON. I hadn't really thought of . . .
JANET. And I love you too, Simon.
SIMON. Thank you.
JANET. I told Mumsie all about you, you know. She has a marvellous instinct on these things. She said—you know what she said?—she said—"That's the man for you, dear." Just like that. Right out.
SIMON. Did she?
JANET. You'll love Mumsie.
SIMON. (*Starts to rise.*) I think I'll open a window.
JANET. (*Pulling him down again.*) Oh no—you're not going to get away from me like that. Oh, Simon . . . I'm just longing to tell Auntie.
SIMON. (*Starts to rise.*) Don't you think it's rather close?
JANET. (*Pulls him down once more*) Stop fidgeting, darling. Auntie doesn't like you, you know. I haven't told her about us of course, . . . but from one or two things she let drop . . .
SIMON. I'm getting a little confused . . . Mumsie—Auntie?
JANET. It's a secret really—but I can tell you. Auntie is Mumsie's sister . . .
SIMON. I won't tell anyone . . .
JANET. That's not the secret bit, silly. You guess who Auntie is (*Moves along sofa* L., *turns to face him.*) go on . . . guess . . .
SIMON. (*Rises, crosses* L.) As far as I'm concerned she might be the Matron . . .
JANET. She is.
SIMON. That's nice. (*Like a scalded cat.*) What! (*Turns violently to face her Comes back to below table.*)
JANET. The Matron She doesn't want anyone to know I'm her niece in case she is accused of favouritism. (SIMON *hurriedly pours himself a large neat gin.*) It doesn't make any difference, does it?

SIMON. Difference? (*Knocks it back and splutters, putting glass down again.*) To what?

JANET. Our arrangements. You know, Auntie said you were the type who was only after one thing. But I knew she was wrong.

(*The phone rings.* SIMON *rushes up round table to phone, which is on the piano.* JANET *moves along to* R. *end of sofa watching him.*)

SIMON. Hello! Oh, Tony . . . Tony . . . No—you haven't interrupted anything . . . No . . . nothing has happened . . . Well . . .

JANET (*Archly.*) Tell the truth and shame the devil.

SIMON. (*In phone.*) Just a sec. (*To* JANET.) What was that?

JANET. (*Rising, and crossing up* R. *of the sofa to his* L *In a hoarse whisper.*) Tell him we're *engaged*.

SIMON. Are we? Oh, yes . . . Couldn't we leave it . . .

JANET. I'll tell him. (*She gets the phone from* SIMON.) This is Janet . . . Simon wanted me to tell you—he's so shy . . . We are engaged to be married . . . No—*engaged.* (*Angrily.*) Well, really! (*She hangs up.*)

SIMON. (*Very weak.*) What did he say?

JANET. He didn't say anything. He just laughed . .

SIMON. He always did have a peculiar sense of humour . . .

JANET. Never mind him, darling. (*Grabbing his hand, she pulls him down to* R. *of sofa.*) D'you know—you haven't kissed me yet?

SIMON. (*Trying to escape* L.) I was just going to suggest that we went . . .

JANET. (*Pulls him to her.*) Come here. You are a shy boy. First you shall kiss me And then I'm going to ring Auntie and tell her the wonderful news.

SIMON. I shouldn't disturb her so late . . .

JANET. She'll be thrilled . . . Now . . . (SIMON *gives*

ACT III   DOCTOR IN THE HOUSE   101

her a quick peck on the cheek) You can do better than that . . . Wait . . . (*She removes her glasses*) Is that better?

SIMON. (*Puts her glasses in his pocket.*) Don't want to break them . . .

JANET. (*Puts both arms round his neck and pulls his head down, kissing him on the lips.*) Now—the phone . . . (*She fumbles her way blindly to in front of drinks cabinet.* SIMON *runs to the phone while she is groping blindly about and quickly wrenches the cable of the phone from its moorings.*) Simon, where is the phone?

SIMON. Here . . .

(*He hands her the phone then collapses on the piano stool, swinging the loose cord in his hand.*)

CURTAIN

SCENE 2

The same. The following evening.

The curtains are closed, all lights are on. The big table is a foot nearer the windows than in the Act I setting The wooden armchair is above it; the chair removed in the last scene back at the R. *side of it. The stool still against the wall. The sofa, too, is a little nearer the table and more up and down stage than in Act I, allowing more space between it and the armchair* D. R. *The small table is behind the sofa again.*

A stricken SIMON *is sitting in the armchair* D. R. VERA *is sitting on the* L. *arm of the armchair beside* SIMON *applying a cold compress to his forehead.* JOHN *is sitting* R. *end of sofa and* TONY *pacing up and down*

TONY. (*Crossing from the pouffe* R. *to* SIMON.) I keep

telling you, you're a clot! A complete and unutterable clot of clots!

VERA Don't keep on at him, Tony.

TONY. He needs a keeper! To walk right into it . . . (*Crossing behind sofa to* L. *end of it*) slap bang into it! Even a mouse tries to avoid a trap—not our Simon: (*Crossing down to pouffe.*) he jumps right in, head first.

JOHN. I warned you about her. We should never have left them alone together last night.

TONY. He's over twenty-one, ain't he? (*Crossing to* L. *of* SIMON) Anyone else—but the Matron's niece! To have old Ironsides as an Aunt-in-Law . . . he might as well shoot himself.

JOHN. You saw the Matron today, Simon?

SIMON. Yes.

TONY Well, what happened?

SIMON (*In a whisper.*) She kissed me.

TONY. How revolting can you get? (*To above armchair.*)

JOHN. Didn't you try to back out?

SIMON. I did drop a hint that I thought we were a bit young for the marriage stakes.

TONY. (*To above sofa.*) Did she bite?

SIMON. With all her teeth. She said that I'd broken the rules by entertaining a nurse in my room, and that she really ought to complain to the Dean.

TONY. (L. *above sofa, round it and down to the pouffe again.*) That would be better than marrying that woman.

SIMON. Would it? If I go up before the Dean once more, it's curtains for me You know that.

JOHN. She's got him over a barrel—right over a barrel.

SIMON. She said she would overlook it, because it was so obviously a case of true love.

(VERA *rises, crosses a step* D. R. *of* SIMON.)

TONY. I want to be sick.

JOHN. (*Rises. Crosses to* D. L. *of* SIMON.) You say the Matron actually kissed you?

SIMON. Don't keep on about it.

TONY. Like being backed-into by an elephant, I should think.

VERA. They say women can talk. Why don't you help him, instead of keeping on?

TONY He is past all human aid.

JOHN. The only thing he can do is fly the country.

TONY. Don't ask me to the wedding! (*Crosses to sofa, sits with feet up, head on* U. S. *arm.*) That's all I ask, as a friend. Don't ask me to be there.

JOHN. Where are you going to hold the ceremony? In a slaughter-house?

VERA. Stop it! (*Crosses to face* JOHN *on his* R.) Once and for all—I won't have it. Poor Simon. Just because he isn't cynical, because he treats women like human-beings —because he's generous and shy (*Crosses to* R. *arm of sofa to face* TONY.) he gets himself into this. It isn't his fault.

(*The door flies open and* SIR LANCELOT *comes charging in.* JOHN *crosses to sofa table, sits* D. S. *end.* TONY *rises.*)

SIR LANCELOT. Where is he? (*To* L. *of sofa.*) Where is that damned young fool? Which of you fellers is my nephew?

SIMON. Here, sir.

SIR LANCELOT. (*Turning to face* SIMON.) You ingrate! You imbecile! You lecherous young villain! What do you mean by it, eh?

(VERA *sits on* R. *arm of sofa.*)

SIMON. It was an accident, sir.

SIR LANCELOT. An accident! (*Picking up the compress from* SIMON'S *forehead, throwing it on the floor.*) On your feet, boy. (SIMON *rises.*) Explain! Explain!

TONY. (*Crossing to* SIR LANCELOT'S L.) He was—er— manoeuvred into it, sir.

SIR LANCELOT. Then he can manoeuvre himself out of it again. (TONY *crosses up to piano, leans on it*. SIR LANCELOT *turns to face* SIMON.) Do you think I'm going to have my family linked with the Matron's? (*To* SIMON.) Have you no sense of decency? No family pride?

SIMON. Yes, sir. I have, sir . . .

SIR LANCELOT. Well, it's an odd way of showing it. (*To* JOHN.) Do you know what I had to contend with this morning? Madam the Matron came into my office simpering—simpering! (*Turning back to* SIMON.) She actually burbled something about the union of our two families. It's the worst thing that's happened to me since I left a swab in Lady Abercrombie!

SIMON. I'm sorry, sir.

SIR LANCELOT. Sorry! Is that all you can find to say? Do you seriously intend to proceed with this unholy and disgusting alliance?

SIMON. Well, sir . . .

JOHN. (*Rising and coming down to* SIR LANCELOT'S L.) He's in a difficult position, you see, sir. If he doesn't, the Matron will get him fired for entertaining a nurse in his lodgings.

SIR LANCELOT. Blackmail, eh?

TONY. Roughly, sir. (TONY *sits on piano stool*. JOHN *returns to sofa table. Sits.*)

SIR LANCELOT. (*To* VERA.) You, woman—get me a drink of some sort.

VERA. (*Rising and crossing to* SIR LANCELOT.) Tea, Sir Lancelot?

SIR LANCELOT. Tea? I said a drink, not a blasted mouth-wash. (VERA *goes up to drinks cabinet, pours a glass of sherry. To* SIMON.) Now, you . . . What's your name again?

SIMON. Simon.

SIR LANCELOT. Simon. Love is an abominable word, but I am forced to use it. Do you love this creature—the Matron's young troll?

SIMON. No, sir, not exactly, sir.

Sir Lancelot. Well, do you or don't you?

Simon. No, sir.

Sir Lancelot. Do you want to marry the wench?

Simon. (*Very definitely.*) No, sir!

Sir Lancelot. Tell me, you haven't got to marry her, have you? (*Nudging* Simon *with his elbow.* Vera *comes down to* Sir Lancelot's L.) Dammit, you haven't got her in the family way?

Simon. Not to my knowledge, sir.

Sir Lancelot. (*Taking the glass of sherry which* Vera *offers him.*) Thank you. Why can't you marry this one? She's attractive enough, isn't she? Why d'you have to pick on the Matron's relations?

Tony. (*Comes down to* L. *of sofa.*) Vera's booked, sir, she's mine!

Sir Lancelot. Yours? God help her! (*He swallows his drink and holds out the empty glass to* Vera.) More, please. I needed that. (Vera *takes glass and returns to drinks cabinet to refill his glass.* Tony *sits on* R. *side of table. To* Simon.) How the devil did you get yourself into this mess, eh?

John (*Rising, coming to* Sir Lancelot's L.) He's not very experienced with women, sir.

Sir Lancelot. You are, I suppose?

John. Well, I know a little about them, sir.

Sir Lancelot. And that's all you ever will know. They're a blasted pest, always getting in the way of a man. (John *returns to sofa table, sits. To* Simon) Oh, you don't look moronic, boy. D'you go round proposing to every girl you meet?

Simon. I didn't propose, sir. She more or less took it for granted.

Sir Lancelot. Didn't you argue?

Simon. I tried to, sir, but she's very forceful!

Sir Lancelot. (*Crosses to sofa, sits* R *end.*) The point is—how can we get you out of it. Any ideas?

Simon. (*Crossing a pace* L.) I'll just have to take my medicine, sir.

SIR LANCELOT. My dear boy, you could marry the bloody Matron herself if I wasn't involved. But I am! I'm not worried about you—you're young and you'll recover. But my position in the hospital will be intolerable if this goes on. The Matron simpering at me round every blasted corner . . . No . . . I will not have it . . .

(*A pause.*)

JOHN. (*Suddenly leans over sofa to* SIR LANCELOT—*very loudly.*) Any ideas, sir?

SIR LANCELOT. (*Jumps.*) Oh, don't frighten me like that, boy. (JOHN *drifts up the sofa to behind* U. S. *end*) Of course I have ideas. The point is—will they work?

SIMON (*Crossing to* R. *of* SIR LANCELOT.) I'm game for anything, sir.

SIR LANCELOT. That is already painfully obvious. (SIMON *away a pace* R. VERA *comes to below sofa table, hands* SIR LANCELOT *a drink over the back of the sofa.*) Thank you. Tell me, is this young lady in your complete confidence?

TONY. Oh, yes, sir. She's one of the family.

SIR LANCELOT. Oh . . . oh, yes. Then listen to me. (JOHN *comes round* U. S *corner of sofa in front of it.* TONY *comes to* JOHN'S L. *putting an arm round his shoulder* VERA *sits on the sofa table and* SIMON *comes in below her.*) There is one possibility . . . but it needs delicate handling—none of this hob-nailed boots stuff. (*A tap at the door.*) Dammit . . .

(SIR LANCELOT *drinks his sherry quickly, handing the glass to* VERA, *who takes it up to the drinks cabinet.* SIMON *goes to open door.* JOHN *goes to above table and sits on it.* TONY *to below table, sits on it.*)

TONY. Come in . . .

(BROMLEY *enters with a bundle of fish and chips and a couple of bottles of beer*)

ACT III DOCTOR IN THE HOUSE

BROMLEY. I brought the supper, sir. (SIMON *closes the door,* BROMLEY *crosses to* R *of* SIR LANCELOT. *To* SIR LANCELOT.) Beg pardon, Sir Lancelot—I didn't know you were here.

(SIMON *to below armchair.*)

SIR LANCELOT. Who the hell are you?
BROMLEY. Bromley, sir.
SIR LANCELOT. I've seen you before.
BROMLEY. That's right, sir—at the hospital.
SIR LANCELOT. I operated on you, didn't I?
BROMLEY. No, sir. There was some talk about it, but you decided to let me live.
SIR LANCELOT. We made a mistake. I can see that now. Well, off you go.
BROMLEY. (*Crosses to* SIMON'S L.) I thought you'd like to know, sir, that your *fiancée* and the Matron are on their way here.

(TONY *rushes to* D. S. *window, opens the curtains and leans out of the window which is open* JOHN *goes to* U. S *window, opens curtains and stands on the window seat, looking out.*)

SIR LANCELOT. Here?
BROMLEY. They was just walking along the street, sir. Looked as though they was coming up here. (*Goes up to drinks cabinet, talks to* VERA.)
SIR LANCELOT. Then this is it. (*Rises.* TONY *comes back to* R. *of table. To* SIMON) You, boy—wait here and greet them. Kiss 'em, if you must. (*Crosses to* TONY.) You have another room here—right . . .
TONY. This way, sir. (*Indicating room* U. L. JOHN *gets down from window seat, opens door* U. L., *switches on light, comes back to above table.*)
SIR LANCELOT. Can you get out to the street without coming back through here?
TONY. There's a fire-escape, sir.

(TONY *goes off* U. L. JOHN *follows him off.* SIR LANCELOT *comes to* L. *of sofa.*)

SIR LANCELOT. A fire-escape? Admirable . . . (*To* SIMON.) And use your common-sense for once, boy. We may be able to save you—but you've got to play your part. (*Starts to go off* U. L., *turns back at* U. S. *corner of sofa when* SIMON *speaks.*)

SIMON. How do you mean, sir?

SIR LANCELOT. Dammit, I haven't time to draw diagrams . . . You keep your eyes skinned—see how the cards are played—and then do your stuff . . . You others —come on . . .

(VERA *crosses to door* U. L. SIR LANCELOT *pushes her off,* BROMLEY *up to door.*)

BROMLEY. Me, too, sir?

SIR LANCELOT. (*Turning in door to* BROMLEY.) Yes . . . come along—don't dawdle, man . . .

BROMLEY. What about the supper, sir?

SIR LANCELOT. What is it?

BROMLEY. Four bits of rock salmon and chips, sir . . .

SIR LANCELOT. Just what I wanted. (*Grabs the packet of chips and goes off followed by* BROMLEY *who closes the door.* SIMON *wanders nervously above sofa. He goes over to bedroom door, opens it slightly. Off, in a roar.*) Go away!

(SIMON *retreats hastily. Crosses down to sofa, bangs the cushions and replaces them. There is a tap at the door, and* SIMON *goes and opens it to admit the* MATRON *and* JANET, *who is now in nurse's uniform.*)

SIMON. Oh, it's you! (*He holds the door wide open.*)

JANET. Why must you always make the same remark when you open the door, Simon, dear? Of course it's me.

(*Comes into the room a few steps.* MATRON *comes in crossing* JANET *to below* R. *arm of sofa.*)

SIMON. Sorry . . . (*Closes the door, comes back to face* JANET *on his* L.)

JANET. Well?

SIMON. Well?

JANET. Simon, darling—really . . . (*She holds her face to be kissed.* SIMON *obliges.*) Now Auntie . . .

SIMON. Auntie—of course . . . (*Crosses gingerly to* MATRON'S R., *is about to peck her cheek when she turns and kisses him noisily on the mouth.*)

MATRON. You've been studying, I hope, Simon.

SIMON. Oh yes . . . been getting down to it. (*He indicates a book lying on the table.*)

(MATRON *crosses to* D. R. *corner of table, picks the book up and replaces it.* SIMON *follows over to her* R.)

MATRON. I know you must be finding it difficult to concentrate with Janet on your mind all the time—but you must.

JANET. (*To below* R. *arm of sofa.*) Auntie has promised to arrange my duties so that I can sit with you during the evenings and help you with your studies.

MATRON. Strictly *entre-nous*, you understand. It would never do for it to get out. But you're one of the family now.

JANET. Not quite, Auntie. (*Crosses to* R. *of* SIMON.)

MATRON. (*Decisively.*) He will be.

JANET. He might have changed his mind.

MATRON. (*Crosses to* SIMON'S L.) Have you?

SIMON. Oh no. Rather not.

(JANET *a pace* R.)

MATRON. (*Crosses to table, sits chair* R. *of it. Facing* D. S.) Good. Now—we came here to tell you to pack your things.

SIMON. Pack? (*A step* L. *to* MATRON.)

MATRON. You don't imagine that I shall allow a nephew of mine to stay here, do you? Of course not. I have found you a room with a friend of mine . . . Angela Butt. She used to be a matron herself, so you'll get on with her. She's promised to keep an eye on you.

JANET. Isn't that simply super, darling?

SIMON. (*Two paces* R. *to* JANET.) I can hardly believe my luck.

MATRON Then that's settled. It will only be temporary, of course—until the wedding. Now—about that. I've been thinking it over, and I think June the ninth will be the most suitable date.

SIMON. (*Pace* L. *to face* MATRON.) Isn't that rather soon?

MATRON. I am not going to ask you to keep your feelings in check for long. I know you young people. No—June the ninth it is. Janet has agreed.

(SIMON *to* R. *of* JANET.)

JANET. Auntie is going to arrange everything, dear. You'll be quite free to concentrate on your work. (*The bedroom door opens and* JOHN, *looking rather dramatic, comes in.*) Oh!

JOHN. (*Coming to* C. *of sofa. Quietly.*) Hello, Janet, I thought I heard your voice.

JANET. (*Crossing* SIMON, *she comes to* JOHN'S R.) Auntie—this is John Evans . . .

(SIMON *to below* R. *arm of sofa.*)

MATRON. I know him.

JOHN. (*To* JANET.) And you, do *you* remember me?

JANET. Naturally.

JOHN. Is it true then? About you and Simon here—my friend, Simon?

JANET. We are going to be married, if that is what you mean.

ACT III   DOCTOR IN THE HOUSE   111

JOHN. Then I am intruding. Excuse me . . . (*He goes to the door,* U. L., *then turns as* SIMON *speaks.*)

SIMON. Don't go, John . . . it's all right.

JOHN. All right? (*Crosses down to below* R. *sofa arm, on* SIMON'S L., *facing front.*) Yes—it's all right for you. But what about me? I suppose I don't count any more.

SIMON. But of course you do, old chap. What on earth is the matter?

JOHN. (*Clicks his tongue very rapidly, winking at* SIMON.) I should ask Janet that question.

MATRON. Will you tell me what you are talking about?

JOHN. (*A pace to her.*) No. It isn't for me to speak. How could you do it, Janet? (*Sits* C. *of sofa.*) How could you?

JANET. Do what?

JOHN. If you don't wish to speak about it—no matter. Wild horses won't make *me* speak. But just remember this— (*Clasps* JANET'S *hand. She pulls it away.*) I kept *my* word, Janet.

MATRON. Janet—explain.

JANET I don't know what he means.

JOHN (*Rising and standing close to her.*) That afternoon in the linen cupboard. That evening—that evening by the sink in the sluice room.—No, I'm sorry—I said I wouldn't speak about it, and I won't. (*Going to* SIMON *and shaking hands.*) I just wish you joy of her, Simon, that's all.

MATRON What is he saying, Janet? What was that about the sluice room?

JANET. Honestly, Auntie . . .

JOHN. (*Crossing to* R. *of* JANET.) I shan't let you down, Janet. But just before I go, may I, as the unlucky loser, may I just wish you and Simon (*Clasps both her shoulders, lifting her and letting her drop again.*) every happiness? (*He goes quickly into his room.*)

MATRON Is he drunk?

SIMON. I don't think so. Janet, you didn't tell me about you and John.

JANET. There was nothing to tell. (*Two paces towards* SIMON.) It's some kind of joke.

SIMON. (*Crossing to* R. *of sofa.*) I don't think he was joking, I've never seen him so serious.

JANET. (*Crossing to* SIMON.) But it's preposterous!

MATRON. What does it matter? (*Rising.*) It's all in the past, anyway. I'm sure Simon will forget all about it.

JANET. But there's nothing to forget.

MATRON. If I remember rightly, I had a little fun in the sluice room in my younger days.

(*A tap at the door.*)

SIMON. Come in.

BROMLEY. (*Enters* D. R., *closing door behind him. To below armchair.*) Ah, good evening, miss. Mr. Sam Hepplewhite told me as I might find you here.

JANET. (*Crossing to* BROMLEY's R.) Mr. Hepplewhite?

BROMLEY. Oh, I understand, miss . . . mum's the word, eh? Still, Mr. Sparrow here is a man of the world and he won't take it amiss.

(SIMON *goes up to sofa table, sits on* D. S. *edge.*)

MATRON. (*A pace* D. R.) What do you want, Bromley?

BROMLEY. Beg your pardon, ma'am, but I've come on rather an important errand for Mr. Hepplewhite.

MATRON. And who is he?

BROMLEY. Mr. Hepplewhite? *Sam* Hepplewhite. (*To* JANET.) Can I speak free, miss?

JANET. Well, really . . .

BROMLEY. That's O.K., miss. (*Crossing to* MATRON) 'Fraid I can't say *who* he is, ma'am, seeing as he's a great personal friend of Miss Janet's here. One might almost say an intimate friend.

MATRON. You've never mentioned this to me, Janet.

JANET I don't know a Mr. Hepplewhite, Auntie, honestly I don't.

(BROMLEY *registers "How can you, miss!"*)

SIMON. (*After a pause.*) Well, go on, Bromley. (*Rising.*)

BROMLEY. I know you'll understand, sir. Well, it seems that Mrs. Hepplewhite—that's Mr. Hepplewhite's wife—has found out that a key to the flat is missing. She's kicking up ructions, so Mr. Hepplewhite asked me to find Tootsie . . .

MATRON. (*Outraged.*) Tootsie?

SIMON (*Amused.*) Tootsie!

BROMLEY. Oh, that's Mr. Hepplewhite's pet name for Miss Janet, very affectionate he is. (*Crossing* R. *to* JANET.) Well, he asked me to find you, miss, and ask you to let him have it.

JANET. Have what?

BROMLEY. Only the key, miss. He said you can keep the jewellery. (JANET *looks mystified.*) I mean, I don't suppose you'll be seeing Mr. Hepplewhite again, will you?

MATRON *Have* you been seeing this person, this Hepplewhite?

BROMLEY. Oh, yes, ma'am, every Wednesday and Thursday at five at the flat.

JANET. (*Crossing to* MATRON.) Oh, Auntie, I haven't. Honestly . . .

BROMLEY. No, sorry, miss, last week it was Friday, wasn't it? (*Goes up to* SIMON *indicating it's up to him now, crosses behind armchair and comes down* R. *of it to in front of it.*)

JANET But I don't know anyone named Hepplewhite.

SIMON. (*After a nudge from* BROMLEY.) That's a likely story!

JANET. Simon!

SIMON First John Evans and now Sam Hepplewhite. (*Walks* U. S. *"hurt" to in front of drinks cabinet, facing* U. S.)

JANET. (*Crossing* R. *to* BROMLEY.) It's a joke—a practical joke.

BROMLEY. I tell you what, miss.—I can see it's a bit awkward for you now, like. I'll tell him you'll let him have the key another day.

JANET. But I haven't . . .

BROMLEY. (*Topping her.*) Not to worry, miss. I dare say he'll be able to square his wife somehow.

JANET. But I don't know . . .

(SIMON *turns and comes* D. S *to* R *of sofa.*)

BROMLEY. (*Topping her again*) And may I take this opportunity of wishing you and Mr. Sparrow every happiness? Got to settle down now, eh, miss? (*Opens door.*) Still, you've had your fling, and what a fling! Evening, all. (*Exit.*)

MATRON. Well!

JANET. (*Crossing* L. *to* MATRON.) Auntie, this is some ghastly plot.

MATRON. I think the less you say, my girl, the better. In many respects you appear to take after your father. (*Crossing* R. *to* SIMON) Simon, I hope you'll overlook these youthful indiscretions.

SIMON. I must say this Sam Hepplewhite fellow seems a bit thick.

(*The voices of* TONY *and* VERA *are heard outside the front door.*)

TONY. (*Off.*) But, my pigeon, I couldn't help it. It was all her fault.

VERA (*Off*) *Je peux pas vivre ici, tu m'énerves* (VERA *bursts in followed by* TONY. *The door is left open Crossing to in front of sofa*) If you think you can come running back to me every time you . . .

TONY. (*Following* VERA *to below* R. *arm of sofa.*) Be reasonable. Listen! (*Seeing* JANET.) Oh, *you're* here!

VERA. Yes, and I'm glad I've found you. I've got a message for you. I don't want your cast-offs, d'you understand? Who do you think you are, sending him back to me every time you've finished with him? I don't take shop-soiled goods, thank you.

JANET I must be going mad, I don't know what you're talking about. (*Sits chair* R. *of table.*)

TONY. (*A step* L. *to* JANET.) No good, Janet, old girl, she knows the lot—the works.

VERA. (*To* JANET.) So it's Simon now, is it? Poor Simon, and I suppose in a couple of weeks when you get tired of him as you got tired of Tony, you'll send *him* packing?

MATRON. Tony?

TONY. Tony Grimsdyke—me!

MATRON. (*A step* L. *to* TONY.) *You* have been involved with my . . . with Janet?

TONY. Involved? That's putting it mildly. (*Sits* R. *end of sofa.*)

VERA. (*To* MATRON) I gave him the best years of my life. I gave him *everything*.

MATRON. Really!

VERA I'm not ashamed of it. I loved him, and he loved me until this—this *woman*—came along. (*To* JANET.) *Quelle espèce de chiqué que vous êtes! Vous n'avez pas honte?* (*To* MATRON.) He was going to marry her, that's what he told me, and for the sake of his happiness, his future, I gave him up.

JANET. (*Rising.*) Stop it! It's all lies . . . She is engaged to him . . .

VERA. (*Turning to face* JANET) That would suit your book, wouldn't it? So that you can be free to carry on with Simon . . . (*She steps* U. S *a pace.*)

TONY (*Kneeling up on sofa Prompting* SIMON) I'm sorry, old boy. I tried to keep the truth from you . . .

JANET. (*Crossing below* VERA *to* TONY. VERA *moves to* R. *of table.*) Auntie—they're making it all up . . .

TONY. *Auntie?*

MATRON. Never mind about that now. (*To* SIMON.) If your friends are playing some kind of stupid joke . . .

SIMON. I don't think they're joking. Three men—John Evans, Sam Hepplewhite and now Tony!

TONY. Hepplewhite the bookmaker?!! (*He looks* JANET *up and down incredulously.*)

SIMON. She had the key to his flat.

(SIMON *crosses up* L. *of armchair.* TONY *flops in the sofa, his head* U. S *end, with his feet up.*)

VERA. There—you see?

JANET. Auntie—don't listen . . .

SIR LANCELOT. (*Entering through the open door. Leaving it open, he comes in to* MATRON'S R.) I am afraid she must listen . . .

MATRON. Sir Lancelot—these students have been playing a cruel and malicious practical joke on this young nurse . . .

SIR LANCELOT. Have they, madam? I heard a good deal just now . . . it seemed to me as though they were the victims . . .

MATRON. Do you think I can't see through it all? (*To* SIMON) You think you have been very clever, Simon, but I shall see the Dean first thing in the morning . . .

SIR LANCELOT. Just one moment, madam. The Dean is aware of course that this young lady is your niece?

MATRON. No . . . no, he isn't. But that will make no difference

SIR LANCELOT. (*Crossing* MATRON *and* JANET *to* R. *of* TONY.) I am not so sure. (*To* TONY.) Grimsdyke, (TONY *rises to* SIR LANCELOT'S L.) you would, of course, be prepared to swear that *you* were engaged to this young lady? (*Taking* JANET'S L. *hand and bringing her to him without looking at her.*)

TONY. If necessary, sir. But—well, sir . . . I love her and I am prepared to forget and forgive if she will allow our engagement to stand . . .

(SIMON *goes up to in front of piano.*)

VERA. (*Crossing to* TONY'S L.) Snake! That's the last straw. (*Slaps his face and slams into the bedroom*)

TONY. (*Turning to* JANET, *disregarding the slap*) Will you, Janet, dear?

JANET. Go away . . . (*Crossing to* MATRON'S L)

SIR LANCELOT. Simon, my boy, (SIMON *comes down to between* TONY *and* SIR LANCELOT.) I think we'll go and see the Dean. It seems to me you have a legitimate complaint. And, Grimsdyke, see if you can find these other chaps, Evans and—what's 'is name?—Hepplewhite. We'll get them to tell their story, too.

MATRON. Janet, come along. (*Pulls* JANET *across her to her* R.)

JANET. But, Auntie, what about Simon?

TONY. (*Crosses to* L. *of armchair.*) Never mind about Simon. (*With a theatrical gesture of pleading, hands together.*) Won't you reconsider me?

MATRON. (*To* TONY.) Be quiet! Sir Lancelot, (SIR LANCELOT *turns to face her.*) I should have thought I might have relied on your support in this matter. As I cannot, all I can say is, the sooner your precious nephew passes his finals and leaves St. Swithin's, the better. Good evening! (*She sweeps out dragging* JANET *with her and slamming the door behind her*)

(SIMON *and* TONY *cheer wildly and* SIR LANCELOT *tries to hush them a little, going round to* D S. *end of sofa to in front of sofa table.* TONY *spreads his arms wide,* SIMON *runs to him.* TONY *grasps* SIMON'S *hands and dumps him in the armchair, and goes behind sofa.* VERA *and* JOHN *come in.* VERA *comes to* U. S. *arm of sofa,* TONY *joins her, on her* R. JOHN *goes to the sofa and kneels on it.*)

TONY. They've gone, chaps, the day is ours

SIR LANCELOT. A magnificent performance, boys, magnificent!

SIMON. Phew!

SIR LANCELOT. I don't know what you're puffing and panting about. You did very little, boy.

SIMON. It was all so sudden. If I'd been warned, sir . . .

SIR LANCELOT. Learn to improvise, boy. First principle of success in medicine, improvisation.

JOHN. D'you think the Matron'll be all right now, sir?

SIR LANCELOT. Well, she'll behave like a scalded kangaroo, but she won't go to the Dean . . . too ludicrous for her. (*To* SIMON.) No, you can breathe again, boy, the family honour is safe.

SIMON. Thank you, sir.

SIR LANCELOT. (*To* TONY.) And for heaven's sake get that damned fire-escape cleaned up, will you! Made myself filthy running up and down the blasted thing. (*He moves to the door then turns to* SIMON.) Oh, and here! Here's a prescription. Get it made up. (*He opens the door.*)

SIMON. (*Taking the prescription.*) A pick-me-up, sir?

SIR LANCELOT. No, you damn fool, a cool-you-down. Next time you feel an irresistible impulse to mingle with the opposite sex, take a swig of that. Good day, gentlemen! (*He sweeps out closing the door.*)

(TONY *brings* VERA *across to above sofa, dancing, turning her under his arm.* SIMON *crosses to* R. *of them.*)

TONY (*Sings joyfully.*)
  Rolling home (*Others join in.*) blind drunk,
  Rolling home, blind drunk
  By the light of the silvery moo-oon.
Let's pop out to the pub for a pint. Got to celebrate.

JOHN. A famous victory. We must remember the date —the sixteenth of . . . (*Counts on his fingers.*) Blimey!

TONY. What's up?

JOHN. (*Kneels up over back of sofa to them; they come closer.*) Do you clots realize that it's exactly five weeks today to our finals?

SIMON What? It can't be!

ACT III DOCTOR IN THE HOUSE

JOHN. It jolly well is, you know!

TONY. We shall have to start doing some work . . .

JOHN. I've hardly looked at a book for months . . .

TONY. We've had a bloody good holiday and now we've got to pay for it . . . Into the stocks, my lads. (*Gets a book from drinks cabinet.* SIMON *gets one from the divan and takes it to armchair* D. R., *sits and opens it* JOHN *gets one from piano top, goes to chair* R. *of table, sits and opens it.*) —Heads down . . . (*He blows the dust from Price's* Practice of Medicine.) Over the top and the best of luck . . . Vera, my pigeon—lots and lots of coffee . . . (VERA *kisses* TONY *and makes for the kitchen,* U. R. *Coming to* R. *end of sofa, where he sits.*) No good wasting time on pneumonia, infant diarrhoea or appendicitis—they were asked last time.

JOHN. We ought to look up torulosis.

SIMON. Never heard of it . . .

TONY. What's the dose of digitalis?

SIMON. (*Rapidly.*) Six grains eight-hourly for three doses, followed by three grains three times a day for two days and half that dose four times daily for two days . . .

TONY. Good lad. (*A pause while they all look at their books. Looking up.* TONY *gets up, strolls down to the footlights and addresses the audience.*) You still here? You might as well shove off, you know. We shall be here for hours bashing the old midnight oil. Nice to have met you and all that . . . Be seeing you round . . . (*Goes back to sofa.*) Night . . . (*Back to his book.*)

JOHN. (*Looking up.*) Night . . . (*Back to his book.*)

SIMON. (*Looking up.*) Night . . . (*Back to his book.*)

(*Picture curtain.* SIMON *on floor leaning against armchair* D. R. TONY, *feet up on sofa.* JOHN *sitting* R. *of table. All studying.* VERA *enters* U. R. *with tray holding three mugs of coffee. She goes to each giving them a mug. As she reaches* JOHN)

THE CURTAIN FALLS

PROPERTY PLOT

Furniture:
Divan
Drinks cabinet
Small table
Upright piano and stool
Standard lamp
Corner cupboard

Furniture
Table and three chairs
Sofa and cushions
Upholstered armchair
Two cane-backed chairs
Pouffe
Fitted bookcase

ACT ONE—SCENE ONE

Props.
Books
Microscope
Skull, wearing a tie
Sports gear of all kinds
Dartboard
Various signs and notices
Policeman's helmet
Matches on top of piano
Glasses on top of piano
Telephone
Stethoscope on table

Table lamp
Small statue
Zinc bowl with water
Rugger shirt in it
Copy of *Sporting Life*
Music and newspaper under piano lid
Canvas holdall ⎫
Gray's *Anatomy* ⎬ *Off* R (SIMON)
Raincoat ⎭
Quart bottle of beer and glasses (*off* U R)

ACT ONE—SCENE TWO

Blouse (VERA) *off* U R
Skeleton (BROMLEY) *off* R
Assortment of beer and liquor bottles
Large glass bowl and ladle

Bottle of cooking sherry
Bottle of tomato sauce
Bag of fish and chips ⎫
Bag of sweets ⎬ *Off* R

ACT TWO

Christmas tree
Christmas decorations
Holly
Bowl of fruit on piano
Duffle coat (JOHN) *off* R

Cardboard box of tinsel (VERA) *off* U R
Frock coat and top hat (TONY) *off* R

PROPERTY PLOT

Case containing six scripts and nightdress (BROMLEY) *off* R
Tray of tea (VERA) *off* U R
Grey wig and nightcap in pocket (BROMLEY)

Straw boater (*in cupboard*)
Hat, gloves and cane (SIR L)
Towel (SIR L) *off* U L
Red grease pencil in waistcoat pocket (SIR L)

ACT THREE—SCENE ONE

Tie (SIMON) *off* U L
Cravat in pocket (SIMON)

Glasses (JANET)
Bottle of gin, orange and glasses

ACT THREE—SCENE TWO

Cold compress (VERA)
Fish and chips
Two bottles of beer } (BROMLEY)

Prescription (SIR L)
Tray of coffee (VERA) *off* U R

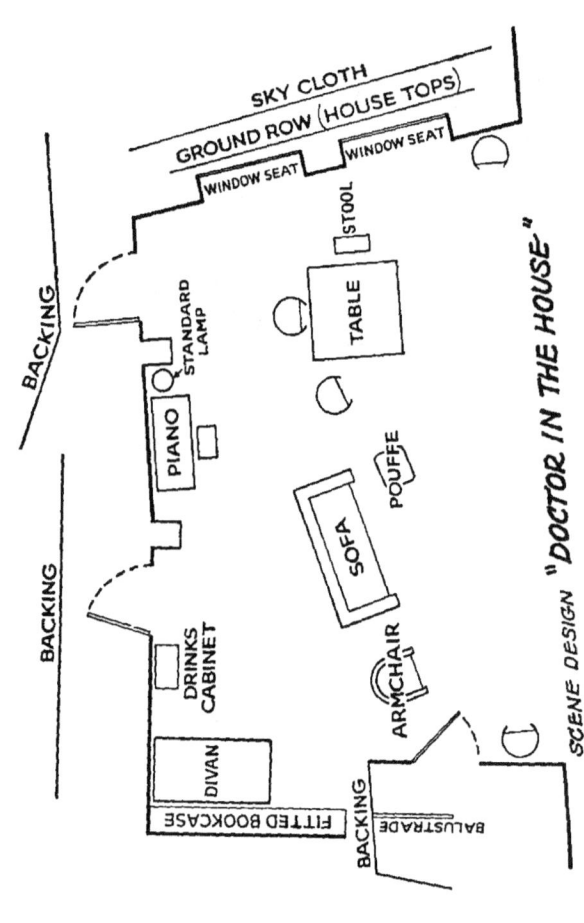

THE OFFICE PLAYS
Two full length plays by Adam Bock

THE RECEPTIONIST
Comedy / 2m., 2f. Interior

At the start of a typical day in the Northeast Office, Beverly deals effortlessly with ringing phones and her colleague's romantic troubles. But the appearance of a charming rep from the Central Office disrupts the friendly routine. And as the true nature of the company's business becomes apparent, The Receptionist raises disquieting, provocative questions about the consequences of complicity with evil.

"...Mr. Bock's poisoned Post-it note of a play."
- New York Times

"Bock's intense initial focus on the routine goes to the heart of *The Receptionist's* pointed, painfully timely allegory... elliptical, provocative play..."
- Time Out New York

THE THUGS
Comedy / 2m, 6f / Interior

The Obie Award winning dark comedy about work, thunder and the mysterious things that are happening on the 9th floor of a big law firm. When a group of temps try to discover the secrets that lurk in the hidden crevices of their workplace, they realize they would rather believe in gossip and rumors than face dangerous realities.

"Bock starts you off giggling, but leaves you with a chill."
- Time Out New York

"... a delightfully paranoid little nightmare that is both more chillingly realistic and pointedly absurd than anything John Grisham ever dreamed up."
- New York Times

SAMUELFRENCH.COM

TREASURE ISLAND
Ken Ludwig

All Groups / Adventure / 10m, 1f (doubling) / Areas
Based on the masterful adventure novel by Robert Louis Stevenson, *Treasure Island* is a stunning yarn of piracy on the tropical seas. It begins at an inn on the Devon coast of England in 1775 and quickly becomes an unforgettable tale of treachery and mayhem featuring a host of legendary swashbucklers including the dangerous Billy Bones (played unforgettably in the movies by Lionel Barrymore), the sinister two-timing Israel Hands, the brassy woman pirate Anne Bonney, and the hideous form of evil incarnate, Blind Pew. At the center of it all are Jim Hawkins, a 14-year-old boy who longs for adventure, and the infamous Long John Silver, who is a complex study of good and evil, perhaps the most famous hero-villain of all time. Silver is an unscrupulous buccaneer-rogue whose greedy quest for gold, coupled with his affection for Jim, cannot help but win the heart of every soul who has ever longed for romance, treasure and adventure.

THE MUSICAL OF MUSICALS (THE MUSICAL!)
Music by Eric Rockwell
Lyrics by Joanne Bogart
Book by Eric Rockwell and Joanne Bogart

2m, 2f / Musical / Unit Set

The Musical of Musicals (The Musical!) is a musical about musicals! In this hilarious satire of musical theatre, one story becomes five delightful musicals, each written in the distinctive style of a different master of the form, from Rodgers and Hammerstein to Stephen Sondheim. The basic plot: June is an ingenue who can't pay the rent and is threatened by her evil landlord. Will the handsome leading man come to the rescue? The variations are: a Rodgers & Hammerstein version, set in Kansas in August, complete with a dream ballet; a Sondheim version, featuring the landlord as a tortured artistic genius who slashes the throats of his tenants in revenge for not appreciating his work; a Jerry Herman version, as a splashy star vehicle; an Andrew Lloyd Webber version, a rock musical with themes borrowed from Puccini; and a Kander & Ebb version, set in a speakeasy in Chicago. This comic valentine to musical theatre was the longest running show in the York Theatre Company's 35-year history before moving to Off-Broadway.

"Witty! Refreshing! Juicily! Merciless!"
- Michael Feingold, *Village Voice*

"A GIFT FROM THE MUSICAL THEATRE GODS!"
– *TalkinBroadway.com*

"Real Wit, Real Charm! Two Smart Writers and Four Winning Performers! You get the picture, it's GREAT FUN!"
- *The New York Times*

"Funny, charming and refreshing!
It hits its targets with sophisticated affection!"
- *New York Magazine*

SAMUELFRENCH.COM

www.ingramcontent.com/pod-product-compliance
Lightning Source LLC
Chambersburg PA
CBHW070644300426
44111CB00013B/2250